STUDENT'S EDITION
GRADE 3

Dr. Cathy Collins Block
Professor of Education
Texas Christian University
and Member, Board of Directors
International Reading Association (2002-2005)

Dr. John N. Mangieri
Director
Institute for Literacy Enhancement

SCHOLASTIC

New York ❀ Toronto ❀ London ❀ Auckland ❀ Sydney
Mexico City ❀ New Delhi ❀ Hong Kong ❀ Buenos Aires

ISBN: 0-439-64045-8

Cover design by James Sarfati
Interior design by Grafica, Inc.
Interior Illustrations by Jackie Snider and Teresa Southwell

Table of Contents

Chapter 1

Chapter 2

Table of Contents

Chapter 3

Chapter 4

CHAPTER 1

Context Clues

Read Words in Context

Vocabulary Words

accident	**hobby**
adventure	**judge**
building	**lawn**
field	**neighbor**
group	**service**

Word Learning Tip!

A **noun** is a word that names a person, place, or thing. A singular noun names one. A plural noun names more than one. Knowing if a word is a noun can help you find the meaning of a new word.

Vocabulary Building Strategy

Use Context Clues When you read, you may come across a word you don't know. Sometimes you can find the meaning of the word by thinking about what the words around it mean. They may give you a clue.

The Case of the Missing Kite

Jay and Maria were best friends and **neighbors**. They lived next door to each other in the same apartment **building.** They ran a detective **service**. Finding things and solving problems for other people was their business.

One afternoon, their friend Anthony came by, very upset.

"Hey, Anthony. What's up?" asked Jay.

"I've lost my kite!" Anthony answered.

"How?" Maria asked.

"I was flying it from the **lawn** in front of my house. Then I had an **accident**. When I tripped and fell, I let go of the string and it flew away. It was a really great kite, too—the best I had ever made. I had worked on it a long time."

Making kites was Anthony's **hobby**, something he liked to do in his free time. Just last year, he had entered a kite-flying contest. The **judge** of the contest gave Anthony first prize.

"Don't worry, Anthony. We'll find it," Maria assured him.

"Okay, now what do we do?" Jay whispered to Maria.

"Let's check which way the wind is blowing," she whispered back. "Then we can figure out in what direction we should look!"

"Look at the leaves in that tree," said Jay. "The wind is blowing that way." He was pointing to the large, grassy **field** where the school soccer team practiced.

The **group** of three friends rushed to the field. They did not have to look long for the kite. "There it is! It's in the tree!" cried Anthony.

"Another job well done, Jay," said Maria.

"Our detective service has solved the problem, and we have had another **adventure**!" added Jay.

Connect Words and Meanings

accident	building	group	judge	neighbor
adventure	field	hobby	lawn	service

Directions Write the letter of the correct meaning in the space before the word. You may use the glossary to help you.

Words		Definition
1. ______	accident	**A.** a large structure with walls and a roof
2. ______	hobby	**B.** an area by a house covered with grass
3. ______	lawn	**C.** something not planned that may cause someone or something to be hurt
4. ______	service	**D.** someone who decides the winner of a contest or whether someone is guilty
5. ______	neighbor	**E.** an exciting time doing something unusual
6. ______	judge	**F.** open land for playing sports or growing crops
7. ______	adventure	**G.** a number of people or things that go together
8. ______	building	**H.** a kind of business or work that helps others
9. ______	field	**I.** a person who lives next door to you or near you
10. ______	group	**J.** something a person does for fun in free time

Create a Hobby Mural Do you have a hobby? Is there something special you like to do in your spare time? On a separate sheet of paper, draw a picture illustrating your hobby. (If you don't have a hobby, make one up.) Under your drawing, complete the following sentence: "I like to _______." Then write two or more sentences using two vocabulary words to describe your hobby. Your teacher can hang your drawings on the wall to create a mural.

Use Words in Context

accident	building	group	judge	neighbor
adventure	field	hobby	lawn	service

Directions Use context clues to choose the best noun from the words you see after each blank. Write the correct noun in the blank.

All winter, Jenna had saved up the money she had earned from her babysitting (**1**) ______________________ (*hobby, lawn, service*). She had used this money to buy seeds and bulbs to plant. Mr. Perez was going to help her plant her garden.

Mr. Perez lived in the (**2**) ______________________ (*field, building, adventure*) next door. He was one of the nicest (**3**) ______________________ (*groups, neighbors, judges*) a person could have. Gardening was his (**4**) ______________________ (*accident, neighbor, hobby*). He grew all kinds of flowers in many different colors. They were all around the edges of the beautiful green (**5**) ______________________ (*lawn, judge, group*).

"Hi, Jenna," Mr. Perez greeted her. "Before we start, let me show you how to use these gardening tools. We don't want a(n) (**6**) ______________________ (*accident, field, hobby*) to happen that will hurt you!"

Then he took Jenna to the small patch of land he had prepared for her by a (**7**) ______________________ (*lawn, adventure, group*) of trees. He showed her how to plant her bulbs and seeds and water them. The two of them worked all morning. "Gee, Mr. Perez!" Jenna cried out. "Maybe I'll enter my flowers in the Garden Contest in the summer. Wouldn't it be great if the (**8**) ______________________ (*neighbor, judge, service*) gave me first prize?"

Create a Round-Robin Story Make up a story with four other children. Decide who will go first, second, and so on. The first child says a sentence, using a vocabulary word or a new noun. For example, *On my way to school, I had a wonderful adventure*. Then the next person builds on the story by saying another sentence, using a vocabulary word or new noun. For example, *I followed a rabbit down a giant hole in the middle of the lawn.*

Put Words Into Action

accident	building	group	judge	neighbor
adventure	field	hobby	lawn	service

Directions The kids at Claremont Elementary School want to raise money for a new school library. Look at the drawings below showing some of the things they are doing. Write vocabulary words to complete the label for each drawing.

1. A car-washing __________ __________________

2. An apartment __________ __________________

3. A __________________ of kids working together

4. Anita mows the grassy __________________

5. Two __________________ who live in the same building

6. A __________________ awards the prize for best pie.

7. Crystal and Sam have the same __________________ : baking.

8. In the __________________ kids race to raise money.

Create a Word Map Choose one of your vocabulary words. On a word map, fill in the titles in the left-hand column: *Name of Word. Describe What It's Like. Give Examples.* Write your ideas in the right-hand column.

Review and Extend

accident	building	group	judge	neighbor
adventure	field	hobby	lawn	service

Learn More!

To change most nouns from **singular** to **plural**, add an *–s*. Sometimes, when a **singular noun** ends with a consonant and *–y*, drop the *–y* and add *–ies*.

Singular Noun *(names one)*	**Plural Noun** *(names more than one)*
house	houses
dog	dogs
hobby	hobbies

Directions Choose a vocabulary word to complete each item. Write it in the blank, using the correct form of the noun. The words in boldface are clues that can help you figure out if the noun should be singular or plural.

1. In her free time, Rima likes to collect shells, paint pictures, and play piano. She has **many different** ______________________ .

2. Adam likes to draw different **kinds of** ______________________ , such as castles, houses, and log cabins.

3. Bo wrote a story for a writing contest. Ms. Tran and Mr. Lee were the **two** ______________________ of the contest.

4. There was a huge snowstorm. Afterwards, Tony built a snow fort from snow that fell on **the** ______________________ in front of **his** house.

5. Derek likes to read about explorers from the past. He wants to know about **their many** exciting ______________________ .

Draw a Cartoon Think about what you and your friends or neighbors like to do when you get together on a Saturday afternoon. For example, you might like to play ball, have a cookout, ride your bikes, or go hiking. On a separate piece of paper, draw a cartoon that shows this activity. Write what people in your cartoon say in thought bubbles. Try to use at least two of your vocabulary words. You can use the singular or plural forms of the nouns.

Check Your Mastery

Directions Read each question. Circle the letter of the best answer.

1. Which of the following is a **hobby**?

A. doing homework
B. helping around the house
C. collecting baseball cards
D. going to sleep

2. Which of the following is a kind of **building**?

A. a desk
B. a barn
C. a book
D. an airplane

3. Where can you see a **lawn**?

A. beside a star
B. in a forest
C. on the bottom of the sea
D. in front of a house

4. What can you do in a **field**?

A. play football
B. shop
C. swim
D. see a movie

5. What would a **judge** at a pie-baking contest do?

A. make pies
B. write about the pies
C. give a prize for the best pie
D. take pictures of all the pies

Directions Read each item. Write the word that best completes it.

6. Before you cross the street, look both ways. That way, you will not have a(n) ______________________ (*accident, adventure, hobby*).

7. When you go on a trip, ______________________ (*lawns, judges, neighbors*) can look after your plants.

8. Dylan wanted to earn money over the summer. He started a lawn-mowing ______________________ (*hobby, service, adventure*).

9. A person who enjoys diving in the deep sea likes to have a(n) ______________________ (*accident, adventure, building*).

10. When many people join hands in a circle, they are a(n) ______________________ (*adventure, accident, group*).

Read Words in Context

Vocabulary Words

accept	**enjoy**
admire	**imagine**
behave	**interrupt**
celebrate	**provide**
discourage	**trust**

Word Learning Tip!

A **verb** is a word that shows actions or feelings. Often, a verb comes right after a noun or pronoun. Sometimes a verb ends in *-s*, *-ed*, or *-ing*. You can use these clues to learn new words.

Vocabulary Building Strategy

Use Context Clues You can find the meaning of verbs you don't know by using the context. Put together the meanings of all the words around an unknown word. This will help you learn a verb's meaning.

Make a Difference Day

Cindy goes to third grade at Central Elementary School. Her heroes are Mrs. Rosa Parks and Dr. Martin Luther King. She **admires** them a lot. Like them, Cindy wants to help build a better world. She wants to make a difference.

Her school has a special day set aside. On this day, students **celebrate** people who made a difference. Children write stories and make posters.

Cindy made a poster for the day. It said, "**Imagine** a better world." It showed children of all races coming together. It showed people **trusting** each other, instead of feeling fear.

The school **provides** food and drinks for the children and their families. Everyone likes to come and have a good time. They **enjoy** getting together with friends and neighbors.

Make a Difference Day isn't just for fun. It is a day for doing good. The school **accepts** gifts for people in need. They hope friends and neighbors will bring canned food, clothing, and books. They **discourage** people from bringing food that will go bad.

How wonderful to see table after table with piles of clothing, canned food, and books. Everyone has given something. They have **behaved** in a way that shows that they want to make a difference.

At three o'clock, the school bell rings and **interrupts** the party. Now it is time to work. Children and parents join together and put all the gifts in bags. Tomorrow they will go to people in need. The gifts will tell them to have hope and dream of a better world.

Connect Words and Meanings

accept	behave	discourage	imagine	provide
admire	celebrate	enjoy	interrupt	trust

Directions Read each definition below. Circle the word that matches each definition.

1. to picture something in your mind

A. trust
B. behave
C. imagine

2. to act properly or well

A. behave
B. accept
C. discourage

3. to take something that you are offered

A. admire
B. accept
C. provide

4. to try to keep people from doing something

A. interrupt
B. discourage
C. celebrate

5. to do something for a special occasion

A. interrupt
B. accept
C. celebrate

6. to stop for a short period of time or to break in when someone else is talking or working

A. admire
B. discourage
C. interrupt

7. to like and respect someone

A. admire
B. accept
C. provide

8. to believe in someone or have confidence in someone

A. accept
B. imagine
C. trust

9. to supply the things someone needs

A. provide
B. celebrate
C. discourage

10. to get pleasure from doing something

A. enjoy
B. admire
C. accept

Play Partner Charades Find a partner. Choose a vocabulary word and act it out. Can your partner guess the word? Then change roles. Try to guess the word your partner acts out.

Use Words in Context

accept	behave	discourage	imagine	provide
admire	celebrate	enjoy	interrupt	trust

Directions Use the vocabulary word in each sentence to write an answer to each question below.

1. Who are two people that you **admire** and respect most and why?

____

2. What is one thing your school could do to **celebrate** on Make a Difference Day?

____

3. What foods do you and your friends **enjoy** eating the most and why?

____

4. Describe the poster and slogan you would **provide** for the Make a Difference Day party. _______________

5. How do you want people to **behave** on your school's Make a Difference Day?

____

6. What three types of gifts will you **discourage** people from bringing and why?

____

7. Who will you **trust** to watch over the gifts? Why did you select this person?

____

8. What might happen to **interrupt** the party or stop it for a short time?

____

Write Three Sentences Write three sentences about something that everyone in your class did in school today. In each sentence, use two verbs. Underline your verbs. Put the sentences in the order in which they happened.

Put Words Into Action

accept	behave	discourage	imagine	provide
admire	celebrate	enjoy	interrupt	trust

Directions Look at each picture. Read the definition. Choose the word from the vocabulary word list that matches. Write it in the blank. Then write a sentence using the word.

Definition: to do something for a special occasion

1. Word: ______________________________

2. My Sentence: ______________________________

____

Definition: to picture something in your mind

3. Word: ______________________________

4. My Sentence: ______________________________

____

Definition: to take something you are offered

5. Word: ______________________________

6. My Sentence: ______________________________

____

Definition: to like and respect someone

7. Word: ______________________________

8. My Sentence: ______________________________

____

Definition: to get pleasure from doing something

9. Word: ______________________________

10. My Sentence: ______________________________

____

Write a Story Write a story about someone you would praise on Make a Difference Day. Use at least five of your vocabulary words. Also use two interesting verbs that add to your story.

Review and Extend

accept	behave	discourage	imagine	provide
admire	celebrate	enjoy	interrupt	trust

Learn More! The ending of a **verb** tells *when* something happens. This is called the **tense**.

Present Tense	Past Tense	Ongoing Action
she walks	she walked	she is walking

Directions Choose the right vocabulary word from the box to fit in the sentence and write it on the blank. A context clue to help you figure out what word to use is printed in boldface type. Add the ending -s, -ed, or -ing to the word you chose. (If the word ends in -e, drop the e before adding -ed or -ing.)

1. Before the event, I **pictured** the day in my mind. I ______________________ everything would go well.

2. My teacher knows she **can depend on me**. She ______________________ me to take care of the little children.

3. On Make a Difference Day, we get a lot of gifts to **give** to the needy. We are ______________________ food and clothing for those in need.

4. The school sent a letter home telling people what to bring. It also **said what people shouldn't bring.** It ______________________ gifts of broken toys and old food.

5. Mr. Garcia and Ms. Arnett stood at the door and **took** the gifts. They ______________________ the gifts that came in.

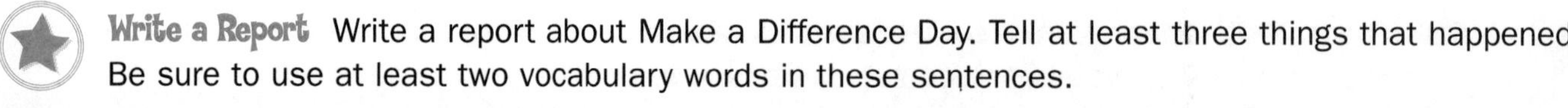

Write a Report Write a report about Make a Difference Day. Tell at least three things that happened. Be sure to use at least two vocabulary words in these sentences.

Check Your Mastery

Directions Read each item below. Write the word that best fits in each blank.

1. You can do many things to __________ (*behave, celebrate, trust*) important events.

2. Can you __________ (*imagine, interrupt, behave*) a world where everyone is happy?

3. I respect and __________ (*provide, admire, imagine*) people who help others.

4. Did you __________ (*accept, enjoy, provide*) the party? I hope you had a good time.

5. Please __________ (*discourage, trust, accept*) this gift. It was all I had to bring.

Directions Complete each sentence below.

6. A cat can **interrupt** your sleep by __________

__________.

7. You can show you **trust** someone by __________

__________.

8. You should **behave** well when __________

__________.

9. You can **discourage** your friends from doing something by __________

__________.

10. You can **provide** treats for a party by __________

__________.

Read Words in Context

Vocabulary Words

bleed/bled	**freeze/froze**
break/broke	**hear/heard**
drink/drank	**shine/shone**
feel/felt	**sweep/swept**
fight/fought	**wear/wore**

Word Learning Tip!

You can form the **past tense** of most verbs by adding *-d* or *-ed*, such as in *decide/decided* or *jump/jumped*. Irregular verbs do not follow a rule. The verbs in this lesson are irregular. Each pair of words shows the present and irregular past tense of a verb.

Vocabulary Building Strategy

Use Context Clues When you read a verb you don't know, be a detective. Look at the words around the unknown word. You might find clues to help you understand what it means!

Travel Back in Time

Imagine you could travel in a time machine! Where would you go? How about going back to the Middle Ages? It was an exciting time of castles, princesses and knights.

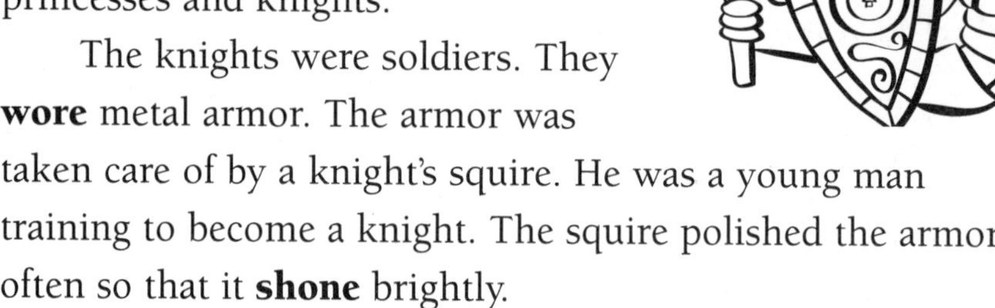

The knights were soldiers. They **wore** metal armor. The armor was taken care of by a knight's squire. He was a young man training to become a knight. The squire polished the armor often so that it **shone** brightly.

Knights wore the metal armor when they **fought** against their enemies in battle. It protected their chest, arms, legs, knees, and feet. Swords and arrows could sometimes go through the metal armor and make the knight **bleed.** The knights hoped that weapons striking their armor would **break** into pieces instead.

Even though you might **hear** stories about how exciting life during the Middle Ages was, it was not easy for everyone. Many people were poor and worked long hours to grow enough food to eat. They grew foods, such as onions and cabbage. These foods, along with nuts and berries, were used to make stews. As a treat, people might sweeten the water they **drank** with honey.

Some families lived in barns with their animals. They were careful to **sweep** their living area with a broom every day to keep it clean. Barns gave little protection from the cold, so people built open fires in the center of their barns. The open fires helped them **feel** warmer. They protected the people and animals so they would not **freeze** in very cold weather.

Connect Words and Meanings

bleed/bled	drink/drank	fight/fought	hear/heard	sweep/swept
break/broke	feel/felt	freeze/froze	shine/shone	wear/wore

Directions Read each definition. In the boxes, write the vocabulary word that fits the definition. You may use the glossary to help you.

1. to listen to
2. to lose blood
3. to swallow a liquid, such as water
4. to damage something so that it is in pieces and no longer works
5. to be dressed in something or have something on
6. to have a sensation or emotion or to touch something
7. to be in a battle or to have an argument
8. to become very cold
9. to polish or rub something to make it bright, or to give off light
10. to clean with a broom or brush

BONUS Look at each vocabulary word to find the numbered letter. Write the letter in the puzzle. You will learn another name for the Middle Ages.

M	1	2	3	1	V	4	5		6	3	M	1	7

Write a Story Work with a partner. Make up a story about the Middle Ages, and write it in your personal word journal. Create characters such as knights, princesses, and village people who live in castles or medieval villages. Try to use at least three vocabulary words and three new verbs.

Use Words in Context

bleed/bled	**drink/drank**	**fight/fought**	**hear/heard**	**sweep/swept**
break/broke	**feel/felt**	**freeze/froze**	**shine/shone**	**wear/wore**

Directions Imagine that you lived in the Middle Ages. Be any person that you want, such as a knight, a princess, or a king. Pretend a reporter asked you questions. Write your answers in the blanks.

1. What kinds of clothes did you **wear**? ____

____.

2. What did you usually **drink** with your meals? ________________________________

____.

3. What kind of stories did you **hear**? ____

____.

4. Did people **freeze** in their castles at night? ________________________________

____

____.

5. Did you **feel** happy about where you lived? Why or why not? __________________

____.

6. What did you **break** when you fell from a horse? ____________________________

____.

7. What objects would **shine** if you polished them? ____________________________

____.

8. What did you use to **sweep** the floor? ______________________________________

____.

Write About Life in a Castle Imagine you live in a castle. Write a few sentences that tell about life in the castle. Ask yourself these questions to help you get started: *What does the castle look like? How big is the castle? Where is it?* Use at least one vocabulary word and one new verb.

Put Words Into Action

bleed/bled	drink/drank	fight/fought	hear/heard	sweep/swept
break/broke	feel/felt	freeze/froze	shine/shone	wear/wore

Directions Look at each pair of sentences. Choose the correct vocabulary word for each sentence from the box. Write the word in the blank. Then answer each question.

break drink

1. Cory and Jake like to ______________________ juice.

2. They hold the glasses carefully so that they do not drop and ____________ .

3. What is the past tense of *break?* ______________________

4. What is the past tense of *drink?* ______________________

froze wore

5. The farmer ______________________ a warm coat in the cold weather.

6. It was so cold that the water in the pond ______________________ .

7. What is the present tense of *froze*? ______________________

8. What is the present tense of *wore*? ______________________

feel sweep

9. When you walk with bare feet, do you ______________________ the dirt on the floor of the barn?

10. You can ______________________ it with a broom.

11. What is the past tense of *feel*? ______________________

12. What is the past tense of *sweep*? ______________________

Write to a Pen Pal Write a letter to someone who lived in the Middle Ages. Tell this person something about your life. You might want to write about your favorite weekend activities, your favorite books, or describe the community where you live. Use at least two vocabulary words.

Review and Extend

bleed/bled	drink/drank	fight/fought	hear/heard	sweep/swept
break/broke	feel/felt	freeze/froze	shine/shone	wear/wore

Learn More!

You can use the present tense to form the future tense. To do this, use the helping verb *will*.

Present Tense	Future Tense	Past Tense
I hear	I will hear	I heard

Directions Read each group of sentences. Choose the pair of vocabulary words that fits. Write the correct form of the verb in each sentence. Then use the future tense of that verb to answer the question.

1. In the Middle Ages, people often ______________________ music at fairs. **2.** Now, people ______________ music on the radio. **3.** Where do you think people will hear music in the future? ____

4. During the Middle Ages, kings and queens ______________________ water from metal cups. **5.** Now, people usually ______________________ water from glasses. **6.** What do you think people will drink from in the future? ______________________
____

7. Long ago, knights often ________________ their enemies using swords. **8.** Today, there are no longer knights who ________________ . **9.** In the future, who do you think will fight battles? ______________________________

10. In the Middle Ages, most people ____________________ their floors with straw brooms. **11.** Now, most people do not ______________________ their floors with brooms, because they use vacuum cleaners. **12.** How do you think people will sweep their floors in the future? ______________________________

Create a Book Character Create a character who likes to travel backward in time. Use the words *Long ago*, or *Once upon a time* to start writing a lively description of your character. Include where your character lives and his or her favorite activities. Use at least two past-tense and future-tense words.

Check Your Mastery

Directions Choose the word that best completes the sentence. Fill in the blank.

1. **Eat** is to **food** as ____________________ (*drink, shine*) is to **water**.

2. **Boil** is to **hot** as ____________________ (*feel, freeze*) is to **cold**.

3. **Eyes** are to **see** as **ears** are to ____________________ (*wear, hear*).

4. **Up** is to **down** as **fix** is to ____________________ (*break, fight*).

5. **Disagree** is to **argue** as **battle against** is to ____________________ (*shine, fight*).

Directions Write the vocabulary word from the box that tells about each group of words.

feel	wear	shine	bleed	sweep

6. hat, shoes, coat — Things to ____________________

7. happy, sad, tired — Ways to ____________________

8. crumbs, dirt, dust — Things to ____________________ up

9. stars, gold, polished shoes — Things that ____________________

10. a cut, a wound, a scratch — Things that might ____________________

Read Words in Context

Vocabulary Words

actual	**general**
complete	**possible**
delicate	**powerful**
delicious	**simple**
extra	**useful**

Word Learning Tip!

An **adjective** describes a noun or pronoun. Usually, an adjective comes right before the noun or pronoun it describes. Sometimes, it comes after a linking verb (*is, are, was, were*). You can use adjectives to tell more about noun or pronoun.

Vocabulary Building Strategy

Use Context Clues You may come across a word you don't know while you are reading. Try this: Look at the words around it for possible clues. Use the clues to help you understand the meaning of the word you don't know.

Daria's Muffin Party

Daria invited her friends Hector, Anthony, and Alana over for a muffin party. She put four muffins on the best plate she could find, and she served them.

Hector took a bite. "This is a **delicious** muffin, Daria. It tastes so good!" he told her.

Next Alana took a bite. "This muffin isn't heavy, like some are. It is very light and **delicate**."

Then Anthony took a bite. "Wow, these muffins have **actual** blueberries in them, not fake ones. Sometimes muffins you get in the store have fake blueberry flavoring."

"How did you make these muffins?" Hector asked. "Just give me a **general** idea. I don't need to hear the entire recipe with all the details."

"Oh, it's not difficult. It's really a very **simple** recipe. I mixed eggs, flour, butter, sugar, and blueberries," Daria explained. "My mom and I used the electric mixer. It's very **powerful**. That's a lot easier than mixing everything by hand with a spoon. A mixer is a very **useful** machine to have. It is very helpful when you have to mix batter."

"I'd love another muffin, Daria. Is that **possible**? Do you have more?" Anthony asked. He had just finished his first one.

"Oh sure!" said Daria. "I have **extra** muffins in the kitchen. You can have as many as you want!"

Daria loved nothing better than to see her friends enjoying something she had cooked. She was pleased. Her muffin party was a **complete** success. Everything was perfect.

Connect Words and Meanings

actual	delicate	extra	possible	simple
complete	delicious	general	powerful	useful

Directions Read the meanings below. Find the correct vocabulary word that matches each meaning. Write the words in the puzzle going across and down. You may use the glossary to help you.

ACROSS

2. in every way, has all the parts needed

6. easy, not hard

8. tasty, very pleasing to taste

9. helpful, can be used a lot

10. very light and pleasant to taste or feel; finely made

DOWN

1. not detailed; applying to many things

3. strong, having great power

4. more than the usual amount

5. might happen or be true

7. real or true

Make Up a Food Ad Think about ideas for a new food product. It could be something you would like to eat or something very unusual—like chili pepper ice cream or pineapple pizza. Then write an advertisement for it. Give the product a name. Write three or more sentences describing it. Make it sound like something people will really want to try. Use at least two vocabulary words and two new adjectives.

Use Words in Context

actual	delicate	extra	possible	simple
complete	delicious	general	powerful	useful

Directions Read each sentence and the three word choices. Write the vocabulary word that fits the definition in boldface. Write the word on the blank.

1. It was **easy** to find the picnic spot. ______________________ *(delicate, simple, general)*

2. The **helpful** signs in the park led them to the spot. ______________________ *(complete, possible, useful)*

3. Everybody wanted to eat a **tasty** sandwich. ______________________ *(actual, delicious, extra)*

4. Kerry likes **more than the usual amount of** mustard on her sandwich. ______________________ *(complete, extra, powerful)*

5. Ben brought his guitar to play. He was careful with it because it was **finely made** and could break easily. ______________________ *(complete, delicate, powerful)*

6. Jessie found a nest with three **real** bird's eggs in it. ______________________ *(actual, simple, useful)*

7. Late in the afternoon, a **very strong** wind blew in. ______________________ *(delicious, powerful, useful)*

8. The teacher made a **basic** announcement **that everyone could understand**. ______________________ *(delicate, simple, general)*

Play the Word Game Write the heading "Things That Are ______" in your personal word journal. Choose one of your vocabulary words to fit in the blank. Then challenge yourself to come up with at least ten items that fit in this category

Put Words Into Action

actual	delicate	extra	possible	simple
complete	delicious	general	powerful	useful

Directions Look at each picture. Choose the best adjective for that picture. Then write the word in the first blank. Next, answer the question. Use the vocabulary word in your answer.

1. a ____________________ and tasty apple to eat for lunch

2. What do you think is good to eat for lunch? ____________________

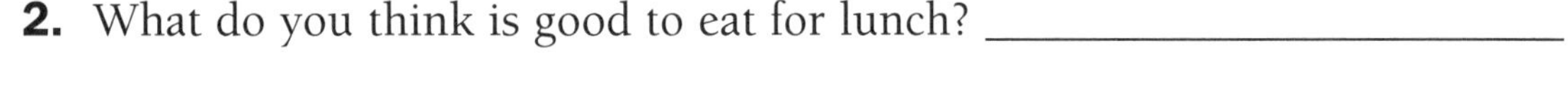

3. a very ________________ map to help you find your way

4. What helps you find your way? ____________________

5. a ____________________ glass horse that could easily break

6. What is something in your house that could break easily?

7. the ____________________ date of the party

8. What is the exact cost of a slice of pizza? ____________________

9. a ____________________ lion with the strength of ten

10. Who is the strongest person you know? ____________________

Create a Word Web In the center circle of the web, write one of your vocabulary words. Then, in the other circles, write all the ideas that come to mind when you think of this word.

Review and Extend

actual	delicate	extra	possible	simple
complete	delicious	general	powerful	useful

Learn More! An adjective usually comes in front of the noun or pronoun it is describing.

I ate a **sweet strawberry.** I picked a **ripe banana.**

An adjective can also come after a linking verb.
The following words are linking verbs: *is*, *are*, *was*, and *were*.

The **strawberry** was **sweet.** This **banana** is **ripe.**

Directions Read each pair of sentences. Use the word clue on the right to figure out the missing adjective for each pair. Write the correct word on the blanks.

CLUES

1. Rick came up with a ____________ plan for celebrating Amy's birthday that did not leave out any details. Rick's plan was ____________ . — **has all the parts it needs**

2. Beth wore a ____________ dress to Amy's party. Beth's dress was ____________ . — **plain**

3. Elena came up with a ____________ solution to the mystery. Elena's solution is ____________ . — **might be true**

4. Malcolm has a ____________ idea of what to do. Malcolm's idea is ____________ , not specific. — **not detailed**

5. Chuck bought ____________ party favors in case he needed them. Four party favors were ____________ . — **more than needed**

Write a Lunch Menu Work with a partner to design and write a lunch menu. Brainstorm favorite lunches. Write brief descriptions in your journal, telling why you like them. Work with your partner to choose five meals for your menu. On a separate piece of paper, design and write your menu. Use at least two vocabulary words and three new adjectives, plus other adjectives you know.

Check Your Mastery

Directions Read each question. Circle the letter of the best answer.

1. Which of the following is **delicious?**

A. a brownie
B. sour milk
C. a teaspoon of medicine
D. a butterfly's wing

2. Which of the following is **powerful?**

A. a basket
B. a car
C. a flower
D. a sheet of paper

3. What can be **useful** when you cook dinner?

A. a broom
B. a map
C. a baking pan
D. a camera

4. Which of these can be **delicate?**

A. a rock
B. an apple
C. someone's touch
D. a trash can

5. Which of the following is **complete?**

A. a broken toy
B. a chair with no legs
C. a full deck of cards
D. a peanut butter and jelly sandwich without jelly

Directions Write the letter of the definition in the blank.

6. _______ actual

7. _______ extra

8. _______ general

9. _______ possible

10. _______ simple

A. easy, not hard

B. real thing or true

C. could happen

D. more than is needed or more than the usual amount

E. not detailed

Read Words in Context

Vocabulary Words

abundant	**grateful**
average	**lonesome**
curious	**popular**
entire	**social**
faraway	**young**

Word Learning Tip!

An **adjective** is a word that describes a noun or a pronoun. It can come before the noun, or after a linking verb. Adjectives can be used to compare two or more things.

Vocabulary Building Strategy

Use Context Clues When you come across a word you don't know, look around it. You may find a clue in the same sentence, the sentence before, or the one after it. Sometimes you may find more than one clue. Put all these clues together. They can help you figure out the meaning of that unknown word!

The King and the Clever Bird

Long ago, there lived an unhappy king. He was very **lonesome** because he had no friends. Being a king, he couldn't mix with ordinary, **average** people. A king can only be friends with royalty, such as queens and princes, but there were no people like that nearby.

The king sat sadly on his throne. "Oh, I wish I could be **popular** and have lots of friends," he sighed.

Just then, a bird flew in the king's window and landed on his arm. "Why are you so sad?" the **curious** bird asked. It wanted to know why the king looked so gloomy. "You have an **abundant** supply of everything you need. There are plenty of beautiful things all around you."

"Oh, you are so right, little bird. I know I should be **grateful** for all that I have—for my castles, my gold, my many jewels. I have an **entire** country that belongs to me—all of it!"

"So what is your problem?" asked the bird.

"I have no **social** life," answered the king. "I never have a good time with other people. All I see are the tops of people's heads as they bow down to me."

Now it so happened that this bird was not only kind but smart, too. "Your highness, I flew here from a distant forest in a **faraway** land. Everyone there is very friendly. You are still **young** and have years to live. Give up your throne and come with me. What good are all your riches when you lack true friends?" asked the bird.

The king's eyes lit up. That night, while everyone slept, he left his kingdom and was never seen there again.

Connect Words and Meanings

abundant	curious	faraway	lonesome	social
average	entire	grateful	popular	young

Directions Circle the letter of the vocabulary word that matches the definition.

1. **Definition:** thankful
   A. social **B.** grateful **C.** average **D.** popular

2. **Definition:** all of something, whole
   A. young **B.** lonesome **C.** faraway **D.** entire

3. **Definition:** sad to be alone; not often visited by other people
   A. curious **B.** lonesome **C.** young **D.** faraway

4. **Definition:** liking to be with other people; friendly
   A. abundant **B.** lonesome **C.** social **D.** average

5. **Definition:** a large number, plenty
   A. popular **B.** young **C.** entire **D.** abundant

6. **Definition:** liked by many
   A. average **B.** popular **C.** lonesome **D.** curious

7. **Definition:** eager to know or find out
   A. curious **B.** social **C.** grateful **D.** abundant

8. **Definition:** not old
   A. entire **B.** faraway **C.** young **D.** average

9. **Definition:** not close, not nearby
   A. faraway **B.** abundant **C.** lonesome **D.** popular

10. **Definition:** ordinary, usual, typical
    A. entire **B.** social **C.** grateful **D.** average

Make Up a Fable or Animal Story With a partner, write a story about an animal who wants some friends. What three things does it do to try to make friends? End your story with a moral.

Use Words in Context

abundant	curious	faraway	lonesome	social
average	entire	grateful	popular	young

Directions Use the clue in the parentheses to write the missing word in the blank.

1. It was just a(n) ______________________ (*plain*) sort of morning at the pond. There was nothing special about it.

2. The pond was ______________________ (*liked by many*) with many animals because it was quiet.

3. The animals were very ______________________ (*friendly*). They liked getting together to have a good time.

4. As the sun rose, the frog said, "I would be ______________________ (*thankful*) if it would rain."

5. Everyone knows that frogs need a(n) ______________________ (*plentiful*) supply of water.

6. Suddenly, there was a loud sound that frightened the ______________ (*baby*) animals.

7. "What could that be?" asked the ______________________ (*eager to know*) turtle.

8. "It sounded like thunder from a ______________________ (*not close*) place," said a duck.

9. After a little while, a huge shadow covered the ______________________ (*whole*) pond.

10. Then a rain cloud said "I was feeling ______________________ (*sad and alone*) so I came down for a visit."

Label the Pond Use colored pencils or crayons to draw a picture of the animals at the pond. Draw arrows to the animals in your picture and write a sentence telling how each animal feels. Use at least three adjectives in the sentences.

Put Words Into Action

abundant	**curious**	**faraway**	**lonesome**	**social**
average	**entire**	**grateful**	**popular**	**young**

Directions Look at the pictures below. Then fill in the blanks in the sentences with the correct vocabulary word.

1. Juan feels ________________________ to his cousin for giving him such a big birthday present.

2. He is very ________________________________ about what is inside the box!

3. Anne never feels ___________________________ when she is playing with her two pals.

4. Sometimes they play for a(n) _______________________ day, from morning to night.

5. No one can say these three are not ______________________, or friendly. They are always together.

Directions Read each question. Then fill in the blank with the correct vocabulary word.

6. What kind of day is like most other days? A(n) ________________________________ day.

7. What is a chicken that has just hatched from an egg? A(n) ______________________ bird.

8. Where do most fairy tales take place? In ____________________________________ places.

Talk About It A fable can teach valuable lessons about life. Here are examples of age-old lessons: *Practice makes perfect. Honesty is the best policy*. In a group, discuss one of these lessons. Tell why the lesson might be useful. Try to use at least two vocabulary words and two new adjectives in what you say.

Review and Extend

abundant	curious	faraway	lonesome	social
average	entire	grateful	popular	young

Learn More! You can use adjectives to compare two or more persons, animals, places, or things.

A rabbit is *faster* than a **turtle.**
Of **all the animals**, the blue whale is the *largest*.

Add *–er* and *–est* to short adjectives that have one syllable. Put *more* and *most* in front of longer adjectives.

Describe one	Compare two	Compare more than two
young	younger	youngest
grateful	more grateful	most grateful

Add *–er* and *–more* when comparing two; add *est* or *most* when comparing three or more.

Directions Read each sentence. Does it describe one? Does it compare two? Does it compare more than two? (The words in bold type give you a clue.) Then look at the adjectives in parentheses ( ). Fill in the blank with the correct form of the adjective.

1. **Ardell** is ______________________ (*young, younger, youngest*) than **his brother**.

2. Some places make you feel all alone. What is the ______________________ (*lonesome, more lonesome, most lonesome*) place you know?

3. **Tess** is ______________________ (*grateful, more grateful, most grateful*) that she can take dance lessons.

4. Which is the ______________________ (*popular, more popular, most popular*) new comedy of the **five**?

5. Who is the ______________ (*social, more social, most social*) person, **Angela** or **Tyrell**?

Make a Gratitude Quilt On a sheet of paper, draw something that makes you feel grateful. Then write two sentences under the picture. Try to use at least one vocabulary word and one new adjective in your sentences. After you have finished, arrange your and others' work on the wall to look like a quilt.

Check Your Mastery

Directions Read each item. Circle the letter of the best answer.

1. You are **grateful**. What do you say?
   A. "Oh, no!" B. "I am sorry." C. "Thank you!" D. "Go away!"

2. What do you call a **young** dog?
   A. a grown up B. a puppy C. a teenager D. a hot dog

3. How does a **lonesome** pet feel?
   A. happy B. sad C. mad D. excited

4. You ate an **entire** sandwich. How much was left over?
   A. half of it B. none of it C. a small piece D. most of it

5. Which of the following is a **social** event?
   A. brushing your teeth B. cleaning your room C. going to a party D. going to sleep

6. Which one is a **popular** treat in the summer?
   A. spinach B. baked potato C. hot soup D. ice cream

7. What might be **abundant** in the night sky?
   A. stars B. flowers C. elephants D. moon

8. What do you do on an **average** day during the week?
   A. go to the dentist B. win a prize C. get a haircut D. go to school

9. Which of the following is a **faraway** place?
   A. the moon B. the lunch room C. your desk D. the street

10. What can you do if you feel **curious** about something?
    A. complain B. forget about it C. ask questions D. sing a song

Read Words in Context

Vocabulary Words

angrily	instantly
easily	only
fiercely	possibly
foolishly	terribly
horribly	wisely

Word Learning Tip!

An **adverb** is a word that tells more about a verb, an adjective, or another adverb. Adverbs tell how, when, where, how often, or how much something happens. Most adverbs end with the letters *-ly*.

Vocabulary Building Strategy

Use Context Clues Sometimes when you read, you will see an adverb that you don't know. Often, you'll find clues if you look at other words in the sentence. You can use the clues to help you find the meaning of the adverb you don't know!

Along the Oregon Trail

(a journal entry from a 10-year-old girl who was on a wagon train traveling from St. Louis, Missouri, to Oregon)

July 8, 1849

We left St. Louis two months ago. The days were bright and sunny until about a week ago. Then the weather changed. It has been **horribly** hot and windy for days now. The wind is blowing the dust everywhere.

Yesterday was **terribly** difficult because of the thick dust. We couldn't see. We were able to travel **only** about one mile. **Wisely,** the wagon master told us to stop for the night. Then all of a sudden, everything got better. The dust storm seemed to stop **instantly**! We saw that we were near a wide river. It was still hot, though!

Finally, it cooled off when the sun went down. Betsy and I decided to sleep outside under the bright stars. But in the middle of the night it rained so **fiercely** that we had to move under the wagon.

It was still raining this morning. Everyone was grumpy. We wondered if the rain would ever stop. Mrs. Winston told us to notice the few small patches of blue sky. "**Possibly** the rain will stop in a few hours," she predicted.

At last the rain did stop! Jed and I ran down to the river to go fishing. As we ran along, we heard Mr. Smith yelling **angrily** at the wagon master. He wanted to know why we couldn't cross the river today. "When people behave **foolishly**, accidents can happen," said the wagon master. "It's smart to wait a few days so the river will get lower. Then we can take the wagons across more **easily** and safely," he said.

I will write again after we cross.

Abigail Lee

Connect Words and Meanings

angrily	fiercely	horribly	only	terribly
easily	foolishly	instantly	possibly	wisely

Directions Read each word and the definitions. Circle the letter of the definition that fits best. You may use the glossary to help you.

1. angrily
- **A.** in a funny way
- **B.** in a loud way
- **C.** in a sleepy way
- **D.** in an upset way

2. easily
- **A.** in a smart way
- **B.** in a way that is not difficult
- **C.** in a happy way
- **D.** in a way that is difficult

3. fiercely
- **A.** in a very strong or violent way
- **B.** in a fast way
- **C.** in a weak way
- **D.** in a gentle way

4. foolishly
- **A.** in a beautiful way
- **B.** in an annoyed way
- **C.** in a way that is not wise
- **D.** in a fearful way

5. horribly
- **A.** in a loud way
- **B.** in an awful way
- **C.** in a wonderful way
- **D.** in a nice way

6. instantly
- **A.** right away
- **B.** later on
- **C.** soon
- **D.** before

7. only
- **A.** at no time
- **B.** not more than; just one
- **C.** more than; many
- **D.** very many times

8. possibly
- **A.** immediately after
- **B.** never happening
- **C.** immediately before
- **D.** perhaps or maybe

9. terribly
- **A.** in a way that is very bad or hard
- **B.** in a weak way; weakly
- **C.** in a thankful way; gratefully
- **D.** in a way that causes laughter

10. wisely
- **A.** in a way that takes a lot of time
- **B.** in a silly way
- **C.** in a smart way
- **D.** in a way that is wishful

Write a Journal Entry Brainstorm with a partner ideas about what a day might be like for you in a wagon train going west. What animals might you see? What chores might you do in the morning before the wagons got started? Then write a journal entry in your personal word journal. Use three vocabulary words and three new adverbs.

Use Words in Context

angrily	fiercely	horribly	only	terribly
easily	foolishly	instantly	possibly	wisely

Directions Read each item and the three vocabulary word choices. Use context clues to figure out which word fits best in the sentence. Then write it in the blank line.

1. The pioneers could take ____________________ (*angrily, foolishly, only*) a few personal items with them. They needed the wagon space for supplies.

2. Pioneers brought food, such as flour, sugar, and corn meal. They had to pack ______________________________ (*terribly, wisely, angrily*) for the long journey.

3. The pioneers could ____________________ (*possibly, terribly, fiercely*) travel 12 miles a day, if oxen were used to pull the wagons.

4. Wagon masters made sure that the drivers stayed on the trail. They did not want people acting ____________________ (*only, wisely, foolishly*) and going off into unmapped land.

5. Rainstorms created mud, which was a big danger for pioneers. One of the oxen could get scared and _______________________ (*horribly, angrily, easily*) hurt if it fell in the mud.

6. Dust storms usually sprang up ____________________________ (*only, foolishly, instantly*) without warning.

7. Strong winds often blew _________________________ (*foolishly, wisely, fiercely*) across the flat plains for days.

8. The winds could be so strong that they could __________________________ (*only, easily, foolishly*) blow over a wagon.

Write a Poem Imagine it's 1852! Write a poem to a friend that describes your wagon train. Use four or more adverbs to describe your trip and underline them.

Put Words Into Action

angrily	fiercely	horribly	only	terribly
easily	foolishly	instantly	possibly	wisely

Directions Read each sentence part. Then choose two vocabulary words that best complete each sentence. Try to use as many different words as possible. You may decide not to use all the words, although you can use some words more than once.

The bear growls—

1. ______________________.

2. ______________________.

The old man speaks—

3. ______________________.

4. ______________________.

The egg breaks—

5. ______________________.

6. ______________________.

The girl laughs—

7. ______________________.

8. ______________________.

The wind blows—

9. ______________________.

10. ______________________.

The boy spent his money—

11. ______________________.

12. ______________________.

Talk to a Scary Animal Imagine that you are sitting around a campfire at night in a wagon circle telling scary stories. Think about scary animals that you might see or sounds that might frighten you. Draw a picture illustrating the scary animal you see. Use speech balloons to show four or more things you would say to make the animal go away. Write a caption for your picture. Try to use at least three vocabulary words and three new adverbs.

Review and Extend

angrily	**fiercely**	**horribly**	**only**	**terribly**
easily	**foolishly**	**instantly**	**possibly**	**wisely**

Learn More! An **adverb** can add meaning to a verb, an adjective, or another adverb. Most adverbs end with the letters *-ly*. You can often change an adjective into an adverb by adding *-ly*.

quiet + ly = quietly *Quiet* means "not loud." *Quietly* means "in a way that is not loud."

Sometimes you change the *y* to *i* to make an adverb. Sometimes you drop the final *e*.

noisy + ly = noisily *Noisy* means "loud." *Noisily* means "in a loud way."
terrible + ly = terribly *Terrible* means "bad." *Terribly* means "in a bad way."

Directions Read each item. Look at the boldfaced adverb. Change the adverb into an adjective. Write the adjective on the blank line. Then write a sentence using both the adverb and the adjective.

1. Claude solved a problem **wisely**. He had a ______________________ solution.

2. Sentence: ____.

3. The clown in the circus acted **foolishly**. The way he behaved was ______________.

4. Sentence: ____.

5. Susan can skate **easily** on the ice. Susan thinks skating is ________________.

6. Sentence: ____.

7. Alan told a **terribly** scary story. All kinds of ______________ things happened in it.

8. Sentence: ____.

9. Will you **possibly** go to camp next summer? It is ______________ that I will go, too.

10. Sentence: ____.

Talk About a Story Work with a partner to complete this story. *Yesterday afternoon, Julia and Allen went to gather berries when suddenly they saw a herd of buffalo in the distance.* Think about what could happen. Then complete the story. Use as many different vocabulary words and new adverbs as possible.

Check Your Mastery

Directions Read the paragraph. Choose the word that fits best and write it on the blank.

People going west took (**1**) ______________________ (*only, instantly, terribly*) about two pounds of tea. Because they needed it to make bread, they (**2**) ______________________ (*horribly, wisely, angrily*) took 200 pounds of flour. Pioneers could (**3**) ______________________ (*possibly, instantly, easily*) use up a lot of flour because they ate a lot of pancakes for breakfast. Even though it was (**4**) ______________________ (*easily, foolishly, terribly*) difficult to carry so much food, the pioneers could not risk running out of supplies. Those who (**5**) ______________________ (*foolishly, wisely, only*) did not take enough dried beans, rice, or dried meat would sometimes have to cut way back on their meals.

Directions Write a sentence to answer each question.

6. What would you wear outside if you saw the rain pounding down on the street **fiercely**?

____

7. What is a favorite activity that you could **possibly** do on a weekend?

____

8. How can you tell when someone speaks **angrily**?

____

9. What might you do **instantly** if someone gave you a present?

____

10. What would you do if a someone behaved **horribly**?

____

Read Words in Context

Vocabulary Words

above	**under**
among	**until**
beneath	**upon**
during	**within**
toward	**without**

Word Learning Tip!

A **preposition** is a word that shows a relationship between a noun and another word in a sentence. Prepositions can show location (where something is), direction (where something is going), and time (when something happens).

Vocabulary Building Strategy

Use Context Clues When you read, you may see a word you don't know. Be a word detective. Look around and see if you can find other words that might help you. Use those words as clues to learn the word you don't know.

Helpful Bugs

Insects, or bugs, are everywhere! They live in the grass, on bushes, and in trees. If you stand in the middle of a bed of flowers, you will probably see butterflies **among** the bright blossoms. If you pick up a rock, you might see a cricket **under** it. There are even insects living **beneath** the ground! Mole crickets, for example, burrow below the soil.

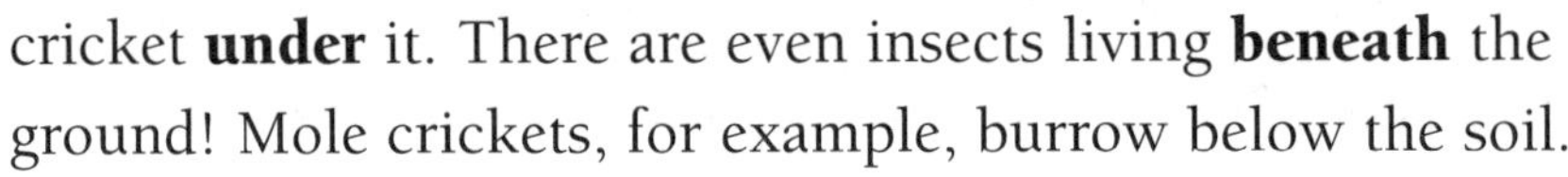

Insects may be small, but many of them are big helpers to people. See that honeybee in the air? It is flying **toward** a flower. After it lands **upon** the flower, it will go into the center of the blossom. While it is **within** the blossom, it will gather the nectar that is inside the blossom. Nectar is the sweet juice of a flower. The bee sucks up the nectar with its long, hollow tongue. A bee will visit many flowers and sip nectar from each one. Then it will fly back to the beehive. There the bees will turn the nectar into honey. **Without** bees, there would be no honey. What a loss that would be!

Look up! There's a ladybug flying **above** you. Ladybugs help farmers. They eat the harmful insects that damage farmers' crops. When the weather starts to get cold, ladybugs have to find places to spend the winter. They crawl into cracks, under leaves, and into pinecones. They stay in these hiding places **during** the winter and sleep **until** the weather gets warmer in the spring. Some ladybugs even hide in the woodwork of houses. Some farmers think it is good luck to have ladybugs in their homes. Would you feel lucky to have a ladybug living with you?

Connect Words and Meanings

above	beneath	toward	until	within
among	during	under	upon	without

Directions Find the word that matches each definition. Write it on the line. You may use the glossary to help you. Use each word only once.

Definition	Word
1. below; less than an amount	_______________
2. lower than, underneath	_______________
3. within a period or span	_______________
4. in the direction of	_______________
5. higher up than, on top of	_______________
6. in the middle of, surrounded by	_______________
7. up to the time of	_______________
8. on	_______________
9. not having, lacking	_______________
10. inside	_______________

Create a Word Web Write the word *insects* in a circle in the middle of your word web. Then write phrases telling where people find insects (such as "on a leaf") in smaller circles around the center circle. Use at least four prepositions.

Use Words in Context

above	beneath	toward	until	within
among	during	under	upon	without

Directions Read each item and choose the word from the three choices that best fits the context. Write that word in the blank.

1. A butterfly looks for a place to lay its eggs. It flies ____________________ a leafy tree.

toward **until** **without**

2. The butterfly carefully lays its eggs ____________________ a nice, wide leaf.

among **upon** **during**

3. A caterpillar grows ____________________ the center of the egg case, safe and protected.

above **toward** **within**

4. When the caterpillar hatches, it is surrounded by food. It certainly won't go hungry ____________________ so many leaves.

among **without** **during**

5. ____________________ all these leaves, the caterpillar would die.

within **without** **during**

6. The caterpillar grows so much that its skin soon splits open. There is a new skin ____________________ its old skin.

beneath **during** **until**

7. This happens several times ____________________ the caterpillar changes into a pupa.

toward **until** **during**

8. The pupa forms a chrysalis around it for protection. It hides itself ____________________ a leaf, safely out of sight.

within **without** **under**

Make an Insect Poster On a sheet of paper, draw an insect you have seen. Under the picture, write a few sentences telling where you saw the insect, how long you watched it, and what it was doing while you watched. Use at least four vocabulary words.

Put Words Into Action

above	beneath	toward	until	within
among	during	under	upon	without

Directions Use the picture as a clue to fill in the blank with the correct vocabulary word.

1. The caterpillar crawls ____________________ the rock.

2. The roly-poly bug hides ________________ or _______________ a leaf.

3. The grasshopper leaps high ___________________ the ground.

4. The spider spins its web ____________________ the flower stalks.

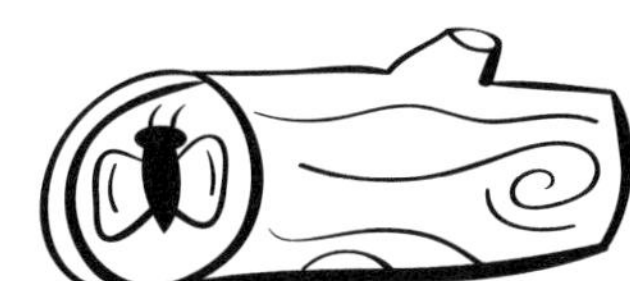

5. The moth hides ___________________ the hollow log.

Directions Sort these prepositions: *above, beneath, during, toward, until*. Write them under one of the headings below.

Where Something Is Located	Where Something Is Going	When Something Happens
6. ____________________	8. _________________	9. ___________________
7. ____________________		10. ___________________

Write a Journal Entry What do you most like to do outdoors? Write a short paragraph for your journal about your favorite outdoor activity. Tell where you go, what you do, and when you do it. Use at least five vocabulary words and new adverbs as well.

Review and Extend

above	beneath	toward	until	within
among	during	under	upon	without

Learn More! A **prepositional phrase** is a group of words that begins with a **preposition** and ends with a noun or pronoun. This noun or pronoun is called the **object** of the preposition. Sometimes the object of the preposition comes right after the preposition.

preposition — object of preposition

There is a big, bright yellow bee **above you.**

prepositional phrase

Sometimes there are a few other words between a preposition and its object.

preposition — object of preposition

A swarm of bees was buzzing **among** the beautifully colored **flowers.**

prepositional phrase

A prepositional phrase includes the preposition, the object of the preposition, and any words that come in between.

Directions Read each question. Underline the prepositional phrase. Then answer the question, using a prepositional phrase.

1. What can you find within a forest?

2. Answer: ______________________________.

3. What can you see above the passing clouds?

4. Answer: ______________________________.

5. What kinds of bugs hide under logs?

6. Answer: ______________________________.

7. How does a day without sunshine feel to you?

8. Answer: ______________________________.

Describe a Walk In your personal journal, write a paragraph about a walk. It can be a real or an imaginary one. Where did you go? What did you see? How long did you walk? Use at least five vocabulary words. Then underline the prepositional phrases in your paragraph.

Check Your Mastery

Directions Read each item. Circle the letter of the preposition that fits best in the blank.

1. We need to divide this pizza _________ the four children.

A. beneath **B.** among **C.** toward **D.** under

2. Trish fell asleep _________ the long, boring movie.

A. upon **B.** within **C.** during **D.** above

3. No children _________ ten years old are allowed on this ride.

A. among **B.** under **C.** upon **D.** without

4. It became lighter outside _________ daybreak.

A. toward **B.** above **C.** beneath **D.** within

5. The cake won't be ready _________ I put the frosting on it!

A. above **B.** upon **C.** during **D.** until

6. Can you see that bird flying high _________ the trees?

A. beneath **B.** within **C.** above **D.** without

7. Plants need water to live and will die _________ it.

A. within **B.** without **C.** beneath **D.** among

8. Did I leave my shoes on the floor _________ the bed?

A. beneath **B.** upon **C.** above **D.** within

9. A lot of snow fell _________ the ground last night.

A. under **B.** among **C.** upon **D.** during

10. The treasure was hidden inside of or _________ the walls of the castle.

A. until **B.** within **C.** during **D.** without

Read Words in Context

Vocabulary Words

after	**likewise**
although	**meanwhile**
before	**otherwise**
finally	**similarly**
however	**therefore**

Word Learning Tip!

Signal words tell when things happen, what causes something to happen, and how one idea in a sentence compares to another idea. A signal word can show the **order** in which something happens. It can explain the **causes** of it or the **effects,** or reasons why something happens. It can **compare and contrast** it to other objects, events, or ideas.

Vocabulary Building Strategy

Use Context Clues When you read, you may see a word you don't know. Be a word detective. Look around and see if you can find other words that might help you. Use those words as clues to understand the word you don't know.

Spaceship Mission: Year 2350

It is the year 2350. All spaceships are driven by robots. These robots speak and follow directions.

All of a sudden, the captain of the robots looks out the spaceship window and yells, "New direction! Turn spaceship!" He sees that the spaceship is speeding towards a large rock moving through space. **Meanwhile**, the robot crew is pushing buttons on the computer. Every robot is trying to turn the spaceship around in time to avoid a collision, or crash. The computer is not working. It is supposed to turn the spaceship away from rocks in its path, not into them.

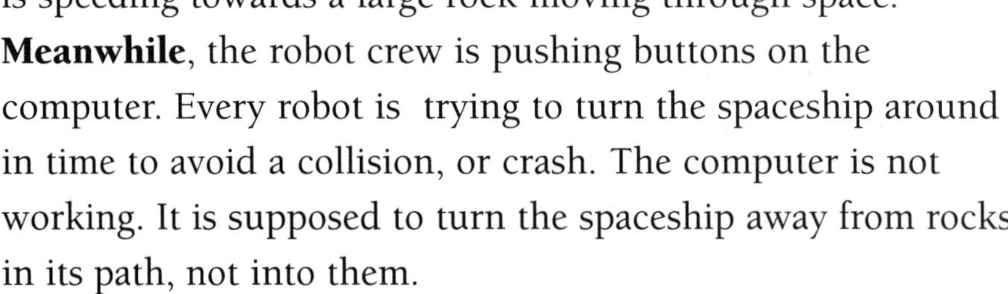

Luckily, one robot pushes the right button. The spaceship slows. **Finally**, it makes a sharp turn, away from the large rock. They are safe at last.

After the ship is safe, Captain Robot Tierney says, "Phew! That was close. We can't let that happen again. **Therefore**, we have to fix the computer right away!"

There had never been a problem like this **before**. The journey from Earth had **otherwise** been a smooth one.

Captain Robot and his crew are headed for Dodi, a planet very far from Earth. The ship has already traveled 70 trillion miles. **However**, they still have a long way to go. They want to find out if people can one day live there. Dodi is a lot like Earth. Earth has water and a sun. **Similarly**, so does Dodi. The sun warms the Earth just the right amount. **Likewise** Dodi's sun does the same. The planets are very much alike, **although** Dodi is bigger.

Connect Words and Meanings

after	before	however	meanwhile	similarly
although	finally	likewise	otherwise	therefore

Directions Read each definition. Circle the letter beside the word that fits the definition. You may use the glossary to help.

1. **Definition:** later than
   A. after **B.** before **C.** likewise **D.** meanwhile
2. **Definition:** in the same way
   A. meanwhile **B.** otherwise **C.** similarly **D.** although
3. **Definition:** earlier or sooner than
   A. after **B.** before **C.** likewise **D.** meanwhile
4. **Definition:** the last, at the end
   A. therefore **B.** although **C.** finally **D.** otherwise
5. **Definition:** in a different way
   A. otherwise **B.** likewise **C.** after **D.** finally
6. **Definition:** at the same time
   A. similarly **B.** meanwhile **C.** after **D.** therefore
7. **Definition:** also, or in the same way
   A. therefore **B.** meanwhile **C.** likewise **D.** otherwise
8. **Definition:** in spite of
   A. although **B.** finally **C.** similarly **D.** meanwhile
9. **Definition:** as a result, for that reason
   A. finally **B.** therefore **C.** otherwise **D.** likewise
10. **Definition:** on the other hand
    A. meanwhile **B.** similarly **C.** therefore **D.** however

Talk About Outer Space With a partner, talk about why people explore outer space. Do you think there may be life on other planets? Try to use at least five vocabulary words and underline them.

Use Words in Context

after	before	however	meanwhile	similarly
although	finally	likewise	otherwise	therefore

Directions Read each sentence and the clue. Write the vocabulary word that best fits in the blank.

1. Angie is in bed now. Earlier, just ________________________ (*before, finally, therefore*) going to bed, she had watched a movie. (*Clue: shows when something happened*)

2. The movie was about an alien from another planet. It took place on a spaceship that had landed on Earth ________________________ (*meanwhile, after, similarly*) traveling through space for 100,000 years. (*Clue: shows when something happened*)

3. The spaceship had run out of fuel. ________________________ (*Therefore, Likewise, However*) it needed to return to Earth. (*Clue: shows the effect, or why something happened*)

4. The spaceship was not as shiny as it once was. ________________________ (*Likewise, Otherwise, Finally*) it was still in good shape. (*Clue: shows a difference*)

5. Angie thought about how the alien looked. ________________________ (*Likewise, Although, Similarly*) its head was very big, it looked a lot like a human. (*Clue: shows a difference*)

6. The alien could communicate, just like humans. ________________________, (*Therefore, However, Likewise*) instead of talking, it sent out thoughts using brain waves. (*Clue: shows a difference*)

7. Humans can walk from one place to another. ________________________, (*Similarly, Otherwise, Finally*) so could the alien. (*Clue: shows how they are the same*)

8. Humans need food to live. ________________________, (*Likewise, After, Therefore*) the alien had to eat to stay alive. (*Clue: shows how they are the same*)

Describe Outer Space Aliens Use your imagination to describe a creature from outer space. Think about what it would look like. How would it be like humans? How would it be different? Write a paragraph describing this creature. Use at least three vocabulary words.

Put Words Into Action

after	before	however	meanwhile	similarly
although	finally	likewise	otherwise	therefore

Directions Read the headings below and then write the vocabulary words in the correct box. In each box, the first letter of each word has been given as a clue.

Words to Compare and Contrast

These words show how things are alike or how they are different.

1. a ____________________ **4.** h ____________________

2. l ____________________ **5.** s ____________________

3. o ____________________

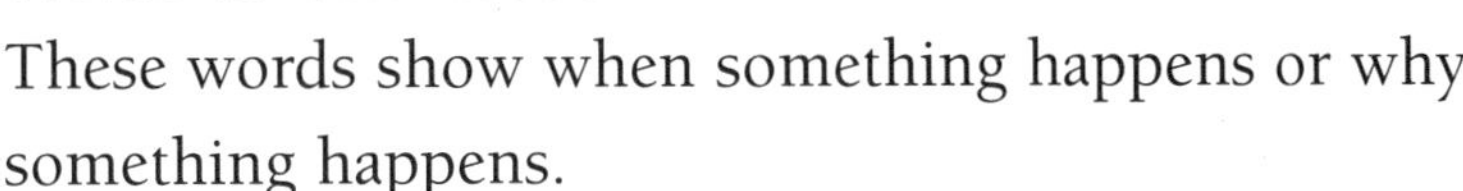

Words to Tell About Time Order

These words show when something happens or why something happens.

6. a ____________________ **9.** b ____________________

7. f ____________________

8. m ____________________

Word to Tell About Cause and Effect

This word tells the result.

10. t ____________________

Interview an Alien In your journal, write three or four interview questions that you would ask an alien. Then, with a partner take turns conducting an interview. As one of you pretends to be an alien, the other will ask questions. Then switch roles. Make sure that each interview question includes one of the vocabulary words.

Review and Extend

after	before	however	meanwhile	similarly
although	finally	likewise	otherwise	therefore

Learn More! Signal words or phrases can show how ideas are related by joining groups of words, complete sentences, or ideas. Here are some other signal words.

time order
first: earliest in time
then: after that
next: right after

cause and effect
because: for the reason that

compare/contrast
but: on the other hand
even though: in spite of
unlike: not like

Directions Look at each item. Use these new boldface signal words as clues to complete each sentence. Choose the vocabulary word that best fits. Write it in the blank.

1. **First**, the rocket took off. **Then** it sped through the sky. ____________________ (*Therefore, Finally, Similarly*) it was in outer space.

2. The planet was too hot **because** it was very close to the sun. The planet was very close to the sun. ____________________ (*Before, Likewise, Therefore*) it was too hot.

3. At sunrise, the sun is in the east, **but** at sunset, it is in the west. The sun rises in the east. ____________________ (*After, Meanwhile, However*), it sets in the west.

4. **Even though** the robot is small, it can do a lot of different jobs. ____________________ (*Although, Otherwise, Therefore*) the robot is small, it can do a lot of different jobs.

5. First, the spaceship landed. **Next**, a strange creature stepped out of it. A strange creature stepped out of the spaceship, ____________________ (*before, after, finally*) it landed.

Write "Into the Future" Stories Science fiction stories often imagine what life will be like in the future. Think about how life might be the same and different in the year 2104. Write a science fiction story in your personal word journal. Try to use at least two vocabulary words and two new signal words.

Check Your Mastery

Directions Read each sentence. Write the word that best fits the sentence in the blank.

1. It was a little cloudy at first, but ____________________ (*likewise, otherwise, therefore*) it was a beautiful day.

2. ____________________ (*Although, Therefore, Otherwise*) the movie was long, it was never boring.

3. Beth likes peanuts. ____________________ (*Therefore, Likewise, Otherwise*), so does Fred.

4. There was a huge snowstorm yesterday. ____________________ (*Although, Meanwhile, Therefore*) there was no school today.

5. Both Kay and Dee can run fast. ____________________ (*However, Therefore, Likewise*) Dee can run faster than Kay.

Directions Pay attention to the vocabulary word in each sentence below. Then, complete the sentence. Write your response on the line.

6. **After** I eat breakfast on Saturdays, I ____

____

7. I waited and waited for my friend. **Finally**, ________________________________

____

8. You should check that you have everything you need **before** ____________________

____

9. I don't like scary movies. **Similarly**, ________________________________

____

10. Dad went shopping at the supermarket. **Meanwhile**, ________________________

____

Read Words in Context

Vocabulary Words

brilliant	**mean**
fork	**mine**
handle	**present**
hide	**press**
lean	**yard**

Word Learning Tip!

Some words have two or more very different meanings. A clue to find the meaning of multiple-meaning words is to see what part of speech it is in a sentence. For example, *bark* can be a verb that means "to make a sharp sound like a dog does" or a noun that means "the tough outer part of a tree."

Vocabulary Building Strategy

Use Context Clues When you come across a multiple-meaning word, a good way to find its meaning is to study the words, phrases, and sentences that surround it. These clues will help you see which meaning of that word is the one that makes sense in the sentence it is in.

Grandpa's Birthday

Today is my Grandpa Mark's birthday. I want to **present** him with something special. I think I'll paint a picture and give it to him.

I know Grandpa likes gardening. He especially likes to grow vegetables in our **yard.** I'll go outside and sit on the grass in the back of the house with my box of watercolors. The colors are so **brilliant.** I have bright blues and greens and oranges. I also have a large white board, a pencil, and brushes.

First I make a pencil sketch of the vegetable. Then I begin to paint. When I am done, I let the painting dry. I wrap it up and put it in a large bag. The bag has a **handle** on it so I can carry it more easily.

Inside Grandpa's birthday card, I put two small dried leaves. Yesterday, Dad showed me how to **press** the leaves to make them flat. I put the card in the bag with the painting.

Dad and I ride our bikes to Grandpa's house. There is a **fork** in the road where it splits, going off in two directions. One way goes to the pond. The other way goes to Grandpa's house.

I watch Grandpa's eyes as he unwraps his gift. He can never **hide** his feelings from me. I can see that he is happy. His eyes light up. "Is this really for me? Is it really **mine**?" he asks. I **lean** over the back of Grandpa's chair to give him a big hug and say, "You **mean** so much to me, Grandpa. You are a very important person in my life. Happy Birthday!"

Connect Words and Meanings

brilliant	handle	lean	mine	press
fork	hide	mean	present	yard

Directions Read each sentence. Then read the two definitions for the boldface word. Circle the letter of the definition that best matches how the boldface word is used.

1. Rita wore sunglasses because the light from the sun was **brilliant**.
   A. very smart
   B. shining very brightly
2. They like to eat with chopsticks instead of a knife and **fork**.
   A. an instrument with prongs used for eating
   B. a place where a road or a river branches in two directions
3. Jake is able to **handle** difficult stunts on a balance beam.
   A. the part used to carry an object
   B. to deal with someone or something
4. The elephant's keeper used a special lotion to keep its **hide** soft.
   A. the skin of an animal
   B. to keep something secret or hidden
5. "Don't **lean** too far over the railing," the guard warned.
   A. slim and muscular; with little fat
   B. to bend over or rest against something
6. People said that Mr. Grisom was a **mean** man, but he was really a kind person.
   A. not kind or nice
   B. to try to say something; intend
7. We explored an old gold **mine** that was no longer in use.
   A. a place beneath the ground where minerals are dug up
   B. belonging to me
8. The mayor will **present** a medal to the brave firefighter.
   A. a gift
   B. to give something to someone
9. The hero was surrounded by the **press** wherever she went.
   A. the people who report the news
   B. to smooth out the wrinkles in something
10. He measured a **yard** of cloth to cover the seat of the chair.
    A. a unit of length equal to three feet
    B. land around a house or building

Write a Riddle Select words from the list. Write a riddle that contains two different meanings for that word. The riddle would be something like this: **What is both smart and bright?** ANSWER: **brilliant.**

Use Words in Context

brilliant	handle	lean	mine	press
fork	hide	mean	present	yard

Directions Fill in the blank in each item. Choose from the following words:

brilliant	hide	present	press	yard

1. Selena is going to ____________________ a dance performance on talent day at school.
2. She has made her own costume out of a ____________________ of striped cloth.
3. She used an iron to ____________________ all the wrinkles out. Then she made a hole in the center of the cloth for her head.
4. She also made a mask in art class. She used the mask to ____________________ her face. No one could see who she was.
5. Selena's costume looked splendid. Everyone agreed that it was ____________________.

Directions Write an answer to each question on the line provided. Show that you understand the meaning of the boldface word.

6. When do you use a **fork**? ____.
7. What do people hope to find in a **mine**? ____.
8. What does it **mean** when someone waves to you? ____.

Write a Letter What project at school have you liked the most? In your personal journal, write a letter to a friend describing that project. Tell what you did and why you liked it. Use at least three vocabulary words.

Put Words Into Action

brilliant	handle	lean	mine	press
fork	hide	mean	present	yard

Directions Read each item below. Use the clues to answer the question, "Who Am I?" Write the vocabulary word that answers the question in the blank.

1. You can use me to describe a dog that is not friendly and to tell the definition of a word. Who am I? ____________________

2. Sometimes I have a fence around me, while others times I have three feet. Who am I? ____________________

3. I'm the student that everyone tries to be and I'm a light that shines too brightly. Who am I? ____________________

4. If you don't like wrinkles you need me, and you listen to me when I report the news. Who am I? ____________________

5. I can help you pick up things, and I can make you to decide which road to take. Who am I? ____________________

6. I am what you do when you give something, and if you are dreaming about something wrapped up and tied with a ribbon, you are hoping for me. Who am I? ____________________

7. A bear has me, and I'm what you may do if you see a bear. Who am I? ____________________

8. I'm what you do when you rest against a wall, and I'm in very good shape. Who am I? ____________________

Write Instructions What activity have you learned to do that you enjoy a lot? For example, did you learn how to throw a basketball or use a computer? Can you grow tomatoes or make pizza? In your personal word journal, write step-by-step instructions for how to do this activity. Use at least two vocabulary words and two other words with multiple meanings.

Review and Extend

brilliant	handle	lean	mine	press
fork	hide	mean	present	yard

Learn More!

Some words have more than one meaning. They can also act as different parts of speech. A ***pun*** is a joke that makes playful use of the different meanings of the same word.

What did the bee say after it stung the child? "I did not *mean* to be *mean*."

The first use of *mean* in this pun is as a verb with the meaning "plan." The second use of *mean* is as an adjective meaning "not nice."

Directions The items below are puns. Fill in the blanks in the sentences that follow the puns with the meaning of the boldface words

What did the gold miner say? "That **mine** is **mine**!"

1. The first **mine** is a noun that means ______________________.

2. The second **mine** is an adjective that means ______________________.

What did the birthday girl say? "Please **present** me with my **present**."

3. The first **present** is a verb that means ______________________.

4. The second **present** is a noun that means ______________________.

What did the door say? "Please **handle** my **handle** with care."

5. The first **handle** is a verb that means ______________________.

6. The second **handle** is a noun that means ______________________.

Make a Word Picture In your personal word journal, use words to describe a place, but don't tell exactly where it is. For example, you could describe a cabin in the forest or a person walking on a busy street. What people and things are in your scene? What are they doing? End your writing with "Where am I?" Try to use as many vocabulary words as you can in your description.

Check Your Mastery

Directions Complete each analogy by choosing the best vocabulary word to write in the blank.

1. **Thick** is to **thin** as **fat** is to ______________________.

lean **brilliant** **press**

2. **Twelve inches** is to a **foot** as **thirty-six inches** is to a ______________________.

present **handle** **yard**

3. **Happy** is to **sad** as **nice** is to ______________________.

brilliant **mine** **mean**

4. **Dim** is to **dull** as **shiny** is to ______________________.

hide **brilliant** **lean**

5. **You** is to **yours** as **my** is to ______________________.

mine **fork** **handle**

Directions Read each question. Circle the letter of the best answer.

6. Which person is a member of the **press?**

A. a garbage collector **B.** an astronaut **C.** a newspaper reporter

7. What do you **hide**?

A. your school **B.** things you don't want others to see **C.** the sun

8. Which of the following do you have to **handle** with care?

A. a large rubber ball **B.** a soft pillow **C.** a glass vase

9. Where are you most likely to find a **fork**?

A. in a kitchen drawer **B.** on the bed **C.** under the sofa

10. How do people usually feel when they get a **present**?

A. mad **B.** sad **C.** happy

Read Words in Context

Vocabulary Words

amusing	**gloomy**
chuckle	**humorous**
comfortable	**laugh**
cozy	**snug**
funny	**uncomfortable**

Word Learning Tip!

Synonyms are words that have the same or nearly the same meaning. *Happy* and *glad* are synonyms because they both mean "feeling good." **Antonyms** are words that have the opposite or nearly the opposite meaning. *Happy* and *sad* are antonyms because *happy* means "feeling good or glad" and *sad* means "feeling bad or unhappy."

Vocabulary Building Strategy

Use Context Clues When you see a word you don't know, look for clues in the surrounding words and sentences. Usually, synonyms and antonyms are written close to each other in a paragraph. The meaning of one of them can be a clue to the meaning of the other one.

Zip and Bessie

Naomi has two pets, Bessie and Zip. Zip is a cat, and Bessie is a dog. Each animal has a favorite spot. Zip likes to lie on his little pillow in a corner of the hallway. He feels very **snug** there, curled up in his comfy little space. Bessie likes to stay outside. She is

comfortable lying on the grass under a tree. The only time she likes to come inside is when it's dark and **gloomy** outside, or when it rains. Bessie is **uncomfortable** when she gets wet. Every time it rains, she happily goes inside and gets **cozy** and warm on her big pillow beside Zip's little one.

Naomi loves Zip and Bessie. They do **amusing** things that make her laugh. Each morning, Zip scratches Naomi's door to wake her up. When Naomi hears him, she **chuckles** and smiles to herself. She knows he's really saying "time to feed me!"

Bessie also makes Naomi laugh. Something **humorous** happened the other day. Bessie loves to go for a drive, and she jumps into the car before anyone else. Naomi and her mom went for a short ride to the post office. When Naomi's mom opened the car door for Bessie to get out, Bessie refused to move. "Come on, Bessie," she urged, "the drive is over." Bessie only tilted her head and gave Naomi's mom a strange look. She seemed to be saying, "Why?" Naomi and her mom had to **laugh** out loud, because Bessie was so **funny.** Finally, they left Bessie in the car, with the door open so she could get out whenever she was ready.

Connect Words and Meanings

amusing	comfortable	funny	humorous	snug
chuckle	cozy	gloomy	laugh	uncomfortable

Directions Fill in the numbered items with the vocabulary words that are either synonyms or antonyms of the words in boldface type. You may use the glossary to help you.

Three synonyms that mean **feeling at ease or relaxed**

1. ______________________

2. ______________________

3. ______________________

An antonym for *comfortable* that means **not feeling relaxed or at ease**

4. ______________________

Three synonyms that mean **causing laughter or smiles**

5. ______________________

6. ______________________

7. ______________________

An antonym for funny that means **dark, depressing, dreary, sad**

8. ______________________

Two synonyms that mean **to make a sound to show that you think something is funny**

9. ______________________

10. ______________________

Create a Pet Treat Think up a new pet treat. Draw a picture of it on a sheet of paper, and then name and describe your invention. What kind of pet is it for? Why would the pet like it? How would the pet use it? Try to include at least three vocabulary words.

Use Words in Context

amusing	**comfortable**	**funny**	**humorous**	**snug**
chuckle	**cozy**	**gloomy**	**laugh**	**uncomfortable**

Directions Help Dexter finish his sentences about his dog, Bart. Use the picture of Dexter and Bart to help you fill in the blanks with the correct vocabulary word.

1. I never feel ______________________ when I'm with my fun-loving dog Bart. (*gloomy, comfortable*)

2. It feels warm and ______________________ when we snuggle close together. (*humorous, cozy*)

3. Bart can be very ______________________ when he does tricks. (*snug, funny*)

4. He makes me ______________________ when he pounces on his favorite toy to fetch it. (*comfortable, chuckle*)

5. I can tell a lot of funny stories about the ______________________ things Bart does. (*amusing, uncomfortable*)

Directions Finish each sentence by filling in the blank with the correct vocabulary word from the box.

comfortable	**snug**	**laugh**	**humorous**	**uncomfortable**

6. If you have to stand in line for a long time, you may feel ______________________ after a while.

7. If you see a clown doing a silly trick, you may ______________________ out loud.

8. If you want to have some fun, try reading a(n) ______________________ comic strip.

Talk About Pet Care Get together with a small group of four or five students. Have a discussion about the kinds of things a pet owner has to do. How does someone take care of a pet? What does a pet need? What mistakes can a pet owner make? Use all the vocabulary words in your discussion.

Put Words Into Action

amusing	comfortable	funny	humorous	snug
chuckle	cozy	gloomy	laugh	uncomfortable

Directions Read each item below. Use the clues to select the correct vocabulary word to write in each blank.

1. This word describes a small room that feels homey and all your own. It rhymes with **rosy**. ________________

2. This word describes how you feel when you are stuck in your room on a rainy day. It rhymes with **roomy**. ________________

3. This word describes how you feel when you pull all the covers on the bed over you. It rhymes with **bug**. ________________

4. This word tells what you do when your uncle tells a funny joke at the dinner table. It rhymes with **buckle**. ________________

5. This word describes a riddle that makes you giggle. It rhymes with **sunny**. ________________

Directions Answer the questions in boldface by writing one of the following words in each of the blanks.

amusing	comfortable	humorous	laugh	uncomfortable

Which two words are synonyms? **6.** ________________ and **7.** ________________

Which two words are antonyms? **8.** ________________ and **9.** ________________

What do you do when you see a very funny movie? **10.** ________________

Create a Word Web Choose a vocabulary word to write in the center circle of the web. Then write five things that the word would describe.

Review and Extend

amusing	comfortable	funny	humorous	snug
chuckle	cozy	gloomy	laugh	uncomfortable

Some **synonyms** have the same meanings, but most have meanings that are similar but not *exactly* the same.

Funny describes something that makes people **laugh** out loud. **Amusing** describes something that makes us smile, but it probably doesn't make us laugh out loud. You might **chuckle** when you see something **amusing**.

If something is **comfortable**, it makes you feel at ease and relaxed. **Cozy** has a warmer feeling than **comfortable**. It suggests something small and warm. A small room with a fireplace is **cozy**. **Snug** also suggests smallness and warmth, but it can describe a tight fit, too. You can feel **snug** in a small space or in something that fits tightly, like a vest.

Directions Complete the sentences by filling in the blank with the vocabulary word that fits best. Be prepared to explain your choice.

1. A ____________________ fire in a small room can make you feel warm and toasty.

2. It's pleasant to sit in a big old ____________________ chair to read.

3. That very ____________________ book made me laugh so hard I almost fell out of my seat.

4. This sweater is a little too tight and ____________________ .

5. My cat is very ____________________ . She makes me smile because she plays all day and gets into trouble.

Find Synonym and Antonym Differences Choose your favorite pair of synonyms or antonyms. Then fold a piece of paper in half. On one half, write one of the words. Then write a paragraph describing a person or animal doing something that fits this word. Use your word as many times as you can. On the other half, do the same thing for the second word.

Check Your Mastery

Directions Read each boldface word. Circle the letter of its synonym or antonym.

1. **gloomy** (antonym)

   A. comfortable B. snug C. difficult D. bright

2. **comfortable** (synonym)

   A. cool B. colorful C. relaxed D. strong

3. **humorous** (antonym)

   A. tight B. precious C. uncomfortable D. serious

4. **funny** (synonym)

   A. laugh B. amusing C. chuckle D. dark

5. **laugh** (antonym)

   A. cry B. smile C. whisper D. joke

Directions Answer each question with a sentence. Make sure your answer shows you understand the meaning of the boldface word.

6. When do you like to feel **snug**?

   ____

7. What would you do if you sat in an **uncomfortable** chair?

   ____

8. Why would you read an **amusing** story?

   ____

9. When might someone **chuckle**?

   ____

10. What can make a room **cozy**?

   ____

Read Words in Context

Vocabulary Words

apart	friendship
chance	hero
common	natural
cooperate	reward
fresh	territory

Word Learning Tip!

In this chapter, you have learned that words from different parts of speech make up sentences. Knowing what part of speech a word is can be one of the clues that helps you understand what an unfamiliar word means. Now, let's put these different kinds of words together!

Vocabulary Building Strategy

Use Context Clues In this chapter, you have learned that using context clues is one way to find the meaning of an unfamiliar word. Context clues are the words and sentences around an unfamiliar word. You can use context clues or the meanings of the words and sentences around a word to help you learn a word's meaning.

The Apple Seed Man

Johnny Appleseed was a real-life American **hero**. He did a lot of good for America. For fifty years, he planted apple seeds every time he could or every **chance** he got. He dreamed about a land where apple trees grew everywhere.

His real name was John Chapman. He was born September 26, 1774, in Massachusetts. He traveled the land throughout much of the American **territory**. This land included Illinois, Indiana, and Ohio. He gathered apple seeds in the fall and planted them in the spring. Whenever he saw rich, good soil, he would plant seeds.

Johnny Appleseed was probably the first person to start nurseries. These were places where people could buy trees. He sold the trees for just a few pennies. If people had no money, they could pay him later. He also let them pay him with used clothing. He worked with pioneers and helped them. He wanted to **cooperate** with them in any way he could, so that they could grow healthy apple trees.

Johnny Appleseed lived a simple life. He ate simple foods, such as **fresh** berries he had just picked and nuts. He liked living alone and being **apart** from other people. He loved the **natural** world where he could be among the trees and wild animals.

Everyone liked him. He enjoyed the **friendship** of both the Native Americans and the new settlers.

What Johnny Appleseed did was not **common**. It was very special. When he died there were about one hundred thousand acres of apple orchards. What a great **reward** for all the good that he did!

Connect Words and Meanings

apart	common	fresh	hero	reward
chance	cooperate	friendship	natural	territory

Directions Match each word with its definition. Write the letter of the definition in the blank space beside each numbered word. Use the glossary to help you.

______	**1.** apart	**A.** to work together for the same purpose
______	**2.** chance	**B.** a brave or good person; the main person in a story
______	**3.** common	**C.** separated, not together
______	**4.** cooperate	**D.** made by nature; normal or usual; not fake
______	**5.** fresh	**E.** the possibility of something happening; an opportunity to do something
______	**6.** friendship	**F.** ordinary, not special in any way
______	**7.** hero	**G.** clean or new; not frozen or canned
______	**8.** natural	**H.** something received for doing something good or useful; to give something to someone who has done a good deed
______	**9.** reward	**I.** being friends; a feeling of warmth towards another person or people
______	**10.** territory	**J.** any large area of land

Name-an-Apple Contest! Work in pairs. Think about different names for a new kind of apple that has just been grown. Write creative slogans and ads to sell this new apple. Try to use at least three vocabulary words in the name of the apple, the slogan, and the ad you create.

Use Words in Context

apart	common	fresh	hero	reward
chance	cooperate	friendship	natural	territory

Directions Read each sentence. Write the word that best fits in the blank.

1. You can buy fruit that is canned or frozen, but there is nothing more delicious than fruit that is ______________________ (*fresh, common, reward*).

2. A mango is a sweet and juicy fruit. If you ever have a ______________________ (*natural, apart, chance*), you should try one!

3. Do you ever put in blueberries when you make pancakes? This is a ______________________ (*common, fresh, natural*) way to make pancakes delicious.

4. My friend Maggie likes to peel a grapefruit and take the sections ______________________ (*apart, cooperate, reward*) so she can eat each piece.

5. When you want a sweet snack, strawberries are a good choice. They have a ______________________ (*common, natural, fresh*) sweetness.

Directions Write your answer to each question in the blank. Use the boldface word in your response.

6. Why is it important to **cooperate** when you are playing team sports?

____

7. Who do you think is a real American **hero**?

____

8. Where are two places that people might form a **friendship**?

____

Create a Friendship Web John Chapman had many friends. Think about what makes people friends, and create a friendship web. Write the word *friendship* in the center of the web. Then, in the other circles, write as many words and sentences as you can describing friendship.

Put Words Into Action

apart	common	fresh	hero	reward
chance	cooperate	friendship	natural	territory

Directions Sort the words. Write each word under the correct heading. The first letter of each word has been given. (One word can be used twice.)

Noun (Naming Word)

1. C ____________________
2. F ____________________
3. H ____________________
4. R ____________________
5. T ____________________

Verb (Action Word)

9. C ____________________
10. R ____________________

Adverb
(Describes Verb, Adjective, Adverb)

11. A ____________________

Adjective (Describes Noun or Pronoun)

6. C ____________________
7. F ____________________
8. N ____________________

Put Parts of Speech Together Select two vocabulary words. Find two other words from other lessons in this chapter that are the same part of speech as the words you chose. Write the best two sentences you can to show that you know the meaning of all four words.

Review and Extend

apart	common	fresh	hero	reward
chance	cooperate	friendship	natural	territory

Learn More!

An *analogy* is made up of two pairs of words. The relationship in the first pair has to be the same as the relationship in the second pair.

Empty is to **full** as **dark** is to **light**.

Empty and *full* are antonyms. Therefore, *dark* and *light* must be antonyms, too.

Easy is to **simple** as **difficult** is to **hard**.

Easy and *simple* are synonyms. Therefore, *difficult* and *hard* have to be synonyms, too.

Directions Complete each analogy. Write the word that best fits in the blank. Then write whether the words in the analogy are *synonyms* or *antonyms*.

1. **Noisy** is to **loud** as **ordinary** is to ________________________ . (*fresh, natural, common*)

2. The words in each pair are ________________________ .

3. **Full** is to **empty** as **together** is to ________________________ . (*natural, apart, fresh*)

4. The words in each pair are ________________________ .

5. **Earth** is to **soil** as ________________________ is to **land**. (*territory, friendship, hero*)

6. The words in each pair are ________________________ .

7. **Bright** is to **shiny** as **new** is to ________________________ . (*fresh, common, natural*)

8. The words in each pair are ________________________ .

Write Analogies Choose two vocabulary words. Write an analogy for each word like the items above. Leave the last word blank. Then give your paper to a partner. See if your partner can complete each analogy.

Check Your Mastery

Directions Read each item below. Write the word that best fits in the blank.

1. Johnny Appleseed liked to wander all over the newly discovered ____________________.

   fresh **territory** **hero**

2. There was always a ____________________ heavy rain might destroy the apple trees.

   common **chance** **cooperate**

3. Children often waited to greet their ____________________ Johnny Appleseed, when he came.

   territory **reward** **hero**

4. Johnny Appleseed did not like to be ____________________ from his apple trees for long.

   chance **apart** **natural**

5. It was very ____________________ for most pioneers to grow apples on their farms.

   common **apart** **cooperate**

Directions Complete each sentence below. Write the answer in the blank.

6. I love the smell of **fresh** ____ .

7. **Friendship** is important because ______________________________________ .

8. The school offered a **reward** to ______________________________________ .

9. I like to **cooperate** with my friends because ____________________________ .

10. The farmer's market sells all **natural** __________________________________ .

Words and Their Parts

Be a Word Architect

Vocabulary Words

misplace	**preschool**
mistreat	**preview**
mistrust	**unannounced**
misunderstand	**unfamiliar**
prepaid	**unimportant**

Word Learning Tip!

When you come to a long word, see if you know the meaning of any parts in the word. Some words are made up of a prefix and a word. A *prefix* is a letter or group of letters added to the beginning of a word. For example, *pre* + *school* = *preschool*. A prefix always has one meaning, no matter what word it is attached to. When you add the meaning of a prefix to other words, you will be able to find the meaning of many new words.

Vocabulary Building Strategy

Use Prefixes A prefix goes in front of a word to form a new word. The meaning of the new word is made up of the meaning of the prefix plus the meaning of the original word. After you add the two meanings together, see if the new meaning makes sense in the sentence.

Learn More!

You know something right away about all words that have the prefix *mis-*. They all include the meaning "bad," "badly," or "wrong." Words with the prefix *pre-* all include the meaning "before." Words with the prefix *un-* all include the meaning "not."

Prefix	Plural Noun	Example
mis-	bad, badly, wrong	misplace
pre-	before	preschool
un-	not	unimportant

Find New Words With Prefixes Look through a magazine or newspaper. Find three new words that have the prefix *mis-*, *pre-*, or *un-*. Write them in your personal word journal. Also write the sentences you find these words in. Then add the new words and the meaning you determined for them to the prefix tree.

Be a Word Architect

misplace	mistrust	prepaid	preview	unfamiliar
mistreat	misunderstand	preschool	unannounced	unimportant

Directions Look at each branch of the prefix tree below. Write each vocabulary word in the blank on the correct branch. Circle the prefix in each word.

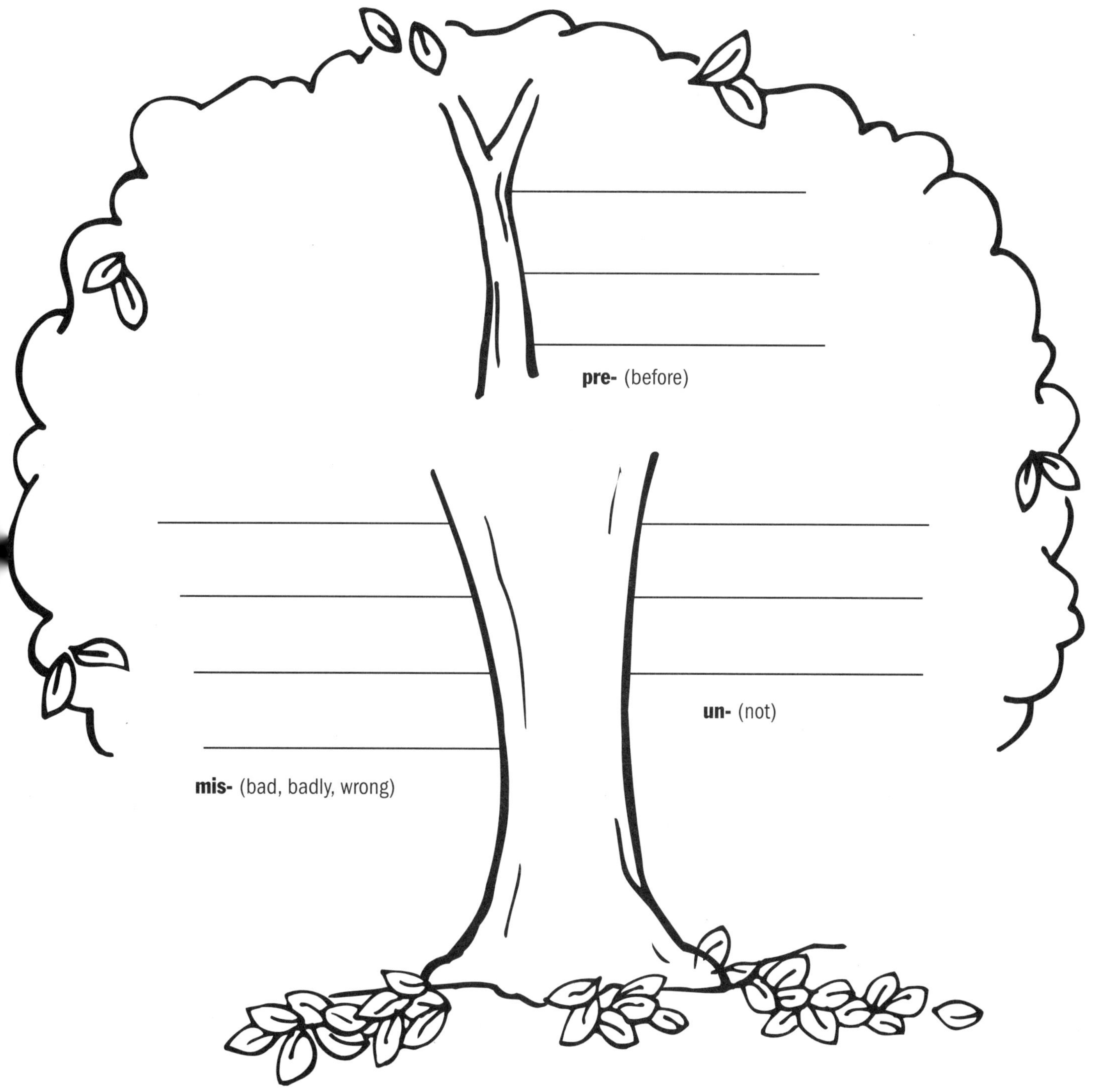

Connect Words and Meanings

misplace	mistrust	prepaid	preview	unfamiliar
mistreat	misunderstand	preschool	unannounced	unimportant

Directions Read the clues. Use them to find the vocabulary word that matches the definition. Write this word in the blank. You may use the glossary or a dictionary to help you.

1. Clue: This word begins with a prefix that means "not."

Clue: It contains a word that means that someone or something has a lot of worth or value.

Definition: not of value or not to be taken seriously ____________________

2. Clue: This word begins with a prefix that means "before."

Clue: It contains a word that means that you gave money to buy something.

Definition: paid for or bought ahead of time ____________________

3. Clue: This word begins with a prefix that means "wrong."

Clue: It contains a word that means "put something somewhere."

Definition: to put something somewhere and then forget where it is ____________________

4. Clue: This word begins with a prefix that means "bad."

Clue: It contains a word that shows that you act toward people or things in a certain way.

Definition: to act badly toward someone or something ____________________

5. Clue: This word begins with a prefix that means "before."

Clue: It contains a word that means "see" or "look."

Definition: something you see ahead of time ____________________

(continued on next page)

Connect More Words and Meanings

misplace	**mistrust**	**prepaid**	**preview**	**unfamiliar**
mistreat	**misunderstand**	**preschool**	**unannounced**	**unimportant**

Directions Continue the activity. Read the clues. Use them to find the vocabulary word that matches the definition. Write this word in the blank. You may use the glossary or a dictionary to help you.

6. Clue: This word begins with a prefix that means "wrong."

Clue: It contains a word that means that you know something or have figured it out.

Definition: to not understand correctly or get the wrong idea ____________________

7. Clue: This word begins with a prefix that means "before."

Clue: It contains a word that names a place people go to learn.

Definition: a school children go to before starting kindergarten ____________________

8. Clue: This word begins with a prefix that means "not."

Clue: It contains a word that means that something is well known.

Definition: not well known or easy to recognize ____________________

9. Clue: This word begins with a prefix that means "wrong."

Clue: It contains a word that means "believe in someone or something."

Definition: to feel a lack of trust in someone or something; feel that something is wrong

____

10. Clue: This word begins with a prefix that means "not."

Clue: It contains a word that means that something was said.

Definition: not named or told about ahead of time ____________________

Write About It Choose six of your vocabulary words. In your personal word journal, write three sentences. Use two vocabulary words in each sentence.

Learn Words in Context

misplace	**mistrust**	**prepaid**	**preview**	**unfamiliar**
mistreat	**misunderstand**	**preschool**	**unannounced**	**unimportant**

September Issue

News Times

50¢

Clowning Around

by Barbara Linde

"Ruth, you're always clowning around!" Ruth Nelson heard that a lot from her parents, her teachers, and her friends. She heard it from the time she was in **preschool**. When Ruth grew up, she did something about it. She became a clown.

Ruth's clown name is "Butterfly." Her costume has a bright red shirt. The pants have big patches on them. She likes to wear buttons that say things like "I Love Animals—Don't **Mistreat** Them," "Take Care of Yourself," and "I Read Books."

Ruth teaches second and third grade at a school in Texas. She does her clowning after school and on the weekends. Every show means a lot to her. She believes that no show is **unimportant**.

Ruth plans her shows carefully. Sometimes she orders things in advance. She writes a check to pay for them ahead of time. The **prepaid** items arrive in the mail. She makes her balloon animals ahead of time, too. She gives her friends a **preview** of the show.

Ruth visits sick children in the hospital. Sometimes, she will tell a child she is coming and sometimes she will visit a child **unannounced**. Ruth says and does silly things. She acts as if she **misunderstands** what she is to do in front of kids. She pretends that people she knows are **unfamiliar**. She pretends to **misplace** something so the children can laugh as she tries to find it.

Ruth puts on shows to make people feel better.

Some children in the hospital are frightened. They **mistrust** the doctors and nurses. But all of the children trust Ruth. "Being a clown is a good way to add happiness and sunshine to the world!" says Ruth.

Use Words in Context

misplace	mistrust	prepaid	preview	unfamiliar
mistreat	misunderstand	preschool	unannounced	unimportant

Directions Write a sentence answering each question. Begin each sentence with the word *Do*. Use a vocabulary word in each sentence.

1. Let others see your act before the big show. What will you let them see ahead of time?

____

2. Where should you visit children who are too young for elementary school?

____

3. Order and pay for balloons ahead of time. What should you have done before they arrive?

____

4. Make kids laugh by showing up at odd times. How should you arrive?

____

5. To get people to laugh, pretend you can't understand what they are telling you.

   What should you make believe you do when someone talks to you?

____

6. Take care of the animals in your act. What should you make sure no one does to them?

____

7. Introduce yourself. What should you do to children who are not familiar?

____

8. What should you do about even those little details that may not seem important?

____

Write New Clown Do's Choose one of the prefixes you have learned in this lesson. In your personal word journal, build new words with this prefix. Then write five new Clown Do's using these words.

Review and Extend

misplace	mistrust	prepaid	preview	unfamiliar
mistreat	misunderstand	preschool	unannounced	unimportant

Directions Read the sentences. Think about the meaning of the prefix in the boldface word. Then fill in the blank

NEW WORDS **misbehave** **preheat** **pretest** **unfamiliar** **unsafe**

1. If Ruth **misplaces** her clown hat, she puts it in the ________________ place and can't remember where it is.

2. If children **misbehave** when Ruth performs, they act ________________ .

3. No child is **unimportant** or ________________ of value.

4. Ruth doesn't let children play with toys that are **unsafe**. She keeps toys that are ________________ safe away from them.

5. Children go to **preschool** ________________ they go to elementary school.

6. On Mondays, children take a **pretest** to find out how much they know about something. They take this kind of test ________________ the regular test.

7. **Preheat** the soup so that it will be ready. Heat it ________________ you need it

8. Ruth saw several **unfamiliar** faces in the crowd. She did ________________ recognize these children since they were new.

Make a Prefix Flower Power Hat Help Ruth make flowers for a clown hat. Choose one of the prefixes. Take a piece of paper. Draw a flower on it with the prefix in the middle. Come up with as many new words with this prefix as you can. Add a petal for each new word. Write the meaning of each new word on the petal, too.

Check Your Mastery

Directions Read each item below. Circle the letter of the choice that best fits the meaning.

1. Everyone wants to feel of value. No one wants to feel _______ .
A. preschool **B.** misplace **C.** unimportant

2. This is what happens when you don't get the idea or point. You _______ something.
A. misplace **B.** misunderstand **C.** unfamiliar

3. If you can't find something, you may have _______ it.
A. mistreated **B.** prepaid **C.** misplaced

4. If you go to someone's house _______ , that person will not know you are coming.
A. unimportant **B.** unannounced **C.** mistreat

5. When you visit a new city, everybody looks _______ to you.
A. preschool **B.** unfamiliar **C.** mistrust

6. You should always be nice to your pets and never _________ them.
A. unfamiliar **B.** preview **C.** mistreat

7. If you don't think someone is honest, you _________ them.
A. mistrust **B.** preview **C.** unannounced

8. Children have fun and learn their ABC's in _________ .
A. misplace **B.** preschool **C.** misunderstand

9. If you gave money for the package ahead of time, you _________ .
A. unfamiliar **B.** unannounced **C.** prepaid

10. We saw a little bit of the movie before it came out. We saw a _________ .
A. preschool **B.** mistreat **C.** preview

Be a Word Architect

Vocabulary Words

acceptable	**likable**
dependable	**responsible**
enjoyable	**sensible**
gentleness	**swiftness**
laziness	**valuable**

Word Learning Tip!

When you come to a long word, see if you know the meaning of any of the parts in that word. Many words are made up of a word and a suffix, which appears at the end of the word. For example, *accept + able = acceptable*. The meaning of a suffix always stays the same no matter what word it is added to. You can use the meaning of a suffix to help find what an unfamiliar word means.

Vocabulary Building Strategy

Use Suffixes A suffix is added to the end of a word. Put together the meaning of the word with the meaning of the suffix to find the meaning of a new word. A suffix can change a word from one part of speech to another.

Learn More!

Suffix	Meaning	Part of Speech
-able, -ible	able to, capable of being,	adjective
-ness	likely to quality of or state of being	noun

When you see a word with the suffix *-able* or *-ible*, you know two things. First, you know that you can use the words "able to, capable of being, or likely to" to find its meaning. Second, you know it's an adjective. So *likable* is an adjective that means "capable of being liked." Of course, you probably would just use another adjective to define the word. You would say that *likable* means "pleasant" or "easy to like."

When you see a word that ends in *-ness*, you know that you can use the meaning of this word part to find an unknown word's meaning. You also know that the word is a noun. So, if someone shows *gentleness*, that person has a gentle quality or is not rough. You might use another noun to define the word. *Gentleness* means "mildness" or "kindness."

Find New Words With Suffixes Look through a book or magazine that you are reading at school. Find at least three new words that have the suffixes *-able*, *-ible*, and *-ness*. Write the new words in your personal word journal, along with a sentence that shows you know its meaning. Then add the words to the Suffix Tree.

Be a Word Architect

acceptable	enjoyable	laziness	responsible	swiftness
dependable	gentleness	likable	sensible	valuable

Directions Look at each branch of the Suffix Tree below. Write each vocabulary word in the blank on the correct branch. Circle the suffix in each word.

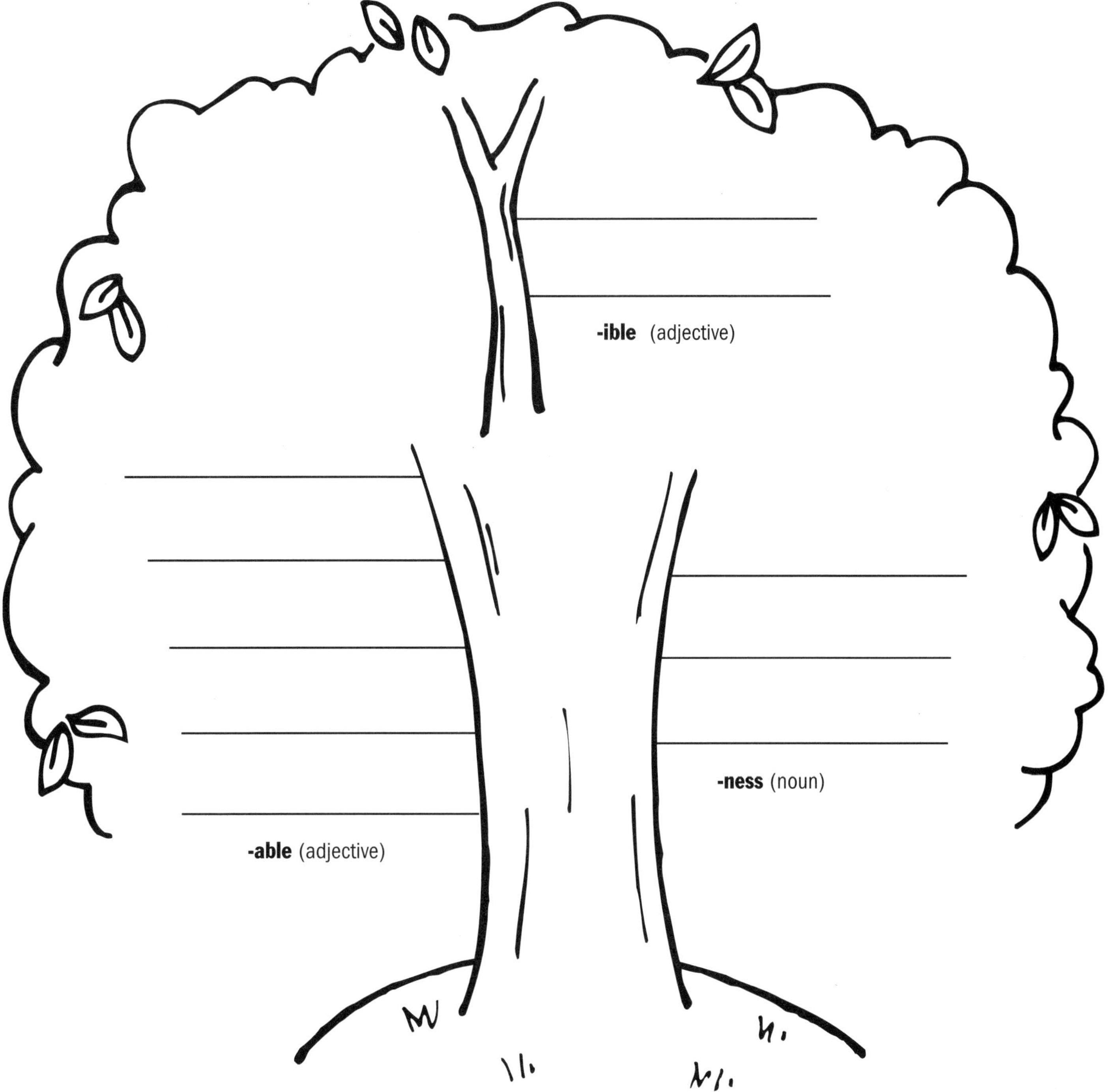

Connect Words and Meanings

acceptable	**enjoyable**	**laziness**	**responsible**	**swiftness**
dependable	**gentleness**	**likable**	**sensible**	**valuable**

Directions Read each definition below. Circle Yes or No to answer each question. Then tell a partner the reason for each answer.

1. **dependable:** an adjective that means able to be depended on

   Is a person who never keeps promises dependable? **Yes** **No**

2. **acceptable:** an adjective that means that someone or something is okay or can be accepted

   Is it acceptable to talk while others are watching a movie? **Yes** **No**

3. **gentleness:** a noun that means kindness, tenderness, and softness

   Would you want a horse to show gentleness if you were learning to ride? **Yes** **No**

4. **sensible:** an adjective that means one thinks carefully and doesn't do silly or dangerous things

   Would a sensible person do something that is very risky? **Yes** **No**

5. **valuable:** an adjective that means that something is worth a lot of money, or is treasured by someone or is important to someone

   Can a fable teach a valuable lesson? **Yes** **No**

6. **laziness:** a noun that names that feeling you have when you don't want to work or do much

   Would you want a person known for laziness to help you with your chores? **Yes** **No**

(continued on next page)

Connect More Words and Meanings

acceptable	**enjoyable**	**laziness**	**responsible**	**swiftness**
dependable	**gentleness**	**likable**	**sensible**	**valuable**

Directions Continue this activity. Read each definition below. Circle Yes or No to answer each question. Then tell a partner the reason for your choice.

7. **enjoyable:** an adjective that means that something or someone gives a lot of pleasure

   Is watching a scary movie enjoyable? **Yes** **No**

8. **likable:** an adjective that means that someone or something is easy to like

   Is a person with a happy smile and cheerful laugh likable? **Yes** **No**

9. **responsible:** an adjective that means that someone is able to be trusted or that someone is to blame for something

   Should the child who is responsible for breaking a window pay for it? **Yes** **No**

10. **swiftness:** a noun that describes the state of being very quick or fast

    Would you want someone who runs with swiftness on the track team? **Yes** **No**

BONUS Write one or two sentences telling about a character in a book you have read or a movie you have seen. Use two vocabulary words. ______________________________

____

____

____

____

Draw a Word Web Choose one of the vocabulary words, such as *likable*. Write it in the center of a word web. Complete the web by writing other words you can think of that have the same suffix as *likable*.

Learn Words in Context

acceptable	**enjoyable**	**laziness**	**responsible**	**swiftness**
dependable	**gentleness**	**likable**	**sensible**	**valuable**

LETTER TO THE EDITOR

Wild Animals Need Places To Live, Too!

Dear Editor:

We learned a **valuable** lesson when the dodo bird disappeared from the earth. Animals need to be protected. People need to take action right now so that more animals don't disappear forever. Wild animals everywhere are losing their homes, because people are moving in where they once lived.

The panda of China and the koala bear of Australia are two animals that are in great danger. They are very **likable** animals. They are **enjoyable** to watch when you see them on TV nature shows. The gorilla of Indonesia is also in danger. It is the largest ape in the world. In movies, gorillas are sometimes shown as mean and scary. The truth is that gorillas are not mean but show **gentleness** to their young and other gorillas in their community. They are known as the gentle giants. They eat mostly leaves and fruits.

The forests where the panda, koala bear, and gorilla live are getting smaller and smaller. People continue to cut down the forests to make towns and build houses. It's time for everyone to act in a more **responsible** way to try to save some land for wild animals. This is no time for **laziness**. People can't just sit back and do nothing! Even though **dependable** people who care about nature are working hard to save these animals, we must all work together. There must be a **sensible** way to solve this problem. We have to act with **swiftness**. If we don't do something soon, these animals may disappear forever from the earth, and that would not be **acceptable**. We cannot let that happen!

Sincerely,
Jeff Griffith

Use Words in Context

acceptable	enjoyable	laziness	responsible	swiftness
dependable	gentleness	likable	sensible	valuable

Directions Complete each sentence. Write the word that best fits in the blank.

1. Dolphins look like they are always smiling. This makes them look very friendly and very ______________________ (*likable, swiftness, laziness*).

2. Cheetahs are the fastest land animals. They are known for their ______________________ (*gentleness, swiftness, responsible*).

3. Elephants are the largest land animals. They are hunted for their ivory tusks. The tusks are ______________________ (*enjoyable, dependable, valuable*).

4. Polar bears move slowly, but it is not because of ______________________ (*laziness, swiftness, sensible*). When they move quickly, they get very hot.

Directions Read each question. Use the boldface word in your answer. Write your sentence in the blank.

5. If you make a plan with a friend, why do you want your friend to be **dependable**?

____

6. Someone left a backpack in the cafeteria. What is the **responsible** thing to do?

____

7. Is it **acceptable** to talk loudly in a library? Why or why not?

____

8. Why is an umbrella a **sensible** item to carry when you know it will rain?

____

Protect an Animal Choose a wild animal you want to see protected. Write a few sentences describing it. Then tell why you want to see it protected. Use at least three vocabulary words and other words with suffixes, too.

Review and Extend

acceptable	**enjoyable**	**laziness**	**responsible**	**swiftness**
dependable	**gentleness**	**likable**	**sensible**	**valuable**

Directions Write an answer to each question below. Use the boldface words in your answer.

1. What animal can show both **gentleness** and **swiftness**?

____

2. Why is it that **dependable** people usually make choices that are **sensible**?

____

3. When is it **acceptable** to show a little **laziness**?

____

4. What type of animals do you find both **likable** and **enjoyable**?

____

Directions Read each new word and its definition. Then write an answer to each question. Use the new word in the answer.

NEW WORDS **kindness** **washable**

5. **kindness:** a noun that means the state or quality or being kind or warm-hearted

   How can you show **kindness** to someone who is new in school?

____

6. **washable:** an adjective that means able to be washed without being damaged

   Why should a soccer uniform be easily **washable**?

____

Write an Animal Poem With a partner, think about an animal you like. Choose two or three new words with suffixes. In your personal word journal, write the words and the animal. Now write a short poem about the animal using those words. Try to use a few vocabulary words.

Check Your Mastery

Directions Write your answer to each question in the blank. Use the boldface word in your answer.

1. What is a **sensible** way to dress on a cold day?

____

2. Where do people keep **valuable** things?

____

3. What is one animal that shows **swiftness** when it moves?

____

4. When do you feel **laziness**?

____

5. Who is more **likable**, a person who smiles or a person who frowns? Why?

____

Directions Read each item below. Write the word that best fits.

6. The Fire Department was ____________________ (*responsible, acceptable, laziness*) for putting out the fire quickly.

7. Going to a party with friends is a lot of fun. It can be a(n)____________________ (*swiftness, laziness, enjoyable*) way to spend time.

8. Our school agreed that having a bake sale was a(n) ____________________ (*swiftness, acceptable, laziness*) way to raise money.

9. The bus always comes on time. The bus driver is very ____________________ (*sensible, dependable, likable*).

10. Mr. Gleason is kind and patient. There is a ____________________ (*acceptable, gentleness, swiftness*) in the way he treats his students.

Be a Word Architect

Vocabulary Words

discovery	rediscover
irreplaceable	renew
newly	renewal
recover	replacement
recovery	undiscovered

Word Learning Tip!

You can learn many long words by looking at the parts that make up the word. If you know the meanings of a word's parts, you have aids that will help you find the meaning of the entire word.

Vocabulary Building Strategy

Use Root Words Sometimes a smaller word forms the base of the longer word. This word is called the root word. When you add the meaning of this word to the meaning of the word parts that come before or after it, you can find the meaning of the longer word. For example, do you see the word *new* in *renewal*? It is formed by adding *re* + *new* + *al*. You can find the meaning of *renewal* by adding the meaning of *new* to the meaning of the prefix *re-* and the suffix *-al*. *Renewal* means "the act of making new again."

Learn More!

Learn Long Words Built From Shorter Words

Word	Meaning
cover	to put something over something else; to conceal or hide
new	just made or begun
place	to put something somewhere

When you see long words that contain the same root word, you know that they have a meaning in common. Look at the words *recover* and *discover*. You know that both words have *cover* as part of their meaning. *Cover* means "to put something over something else or to hide something." When you add *re-* to *cover*, you know that *re-* means "to do again." Therefore, when you *recover* something, you go back to find something again that had been hidden or lost. To find out what *discover* means, you add the meaning of *dis-* to *cover*. *Dis-* means "opposite of" so *discover* is the opposite of hiding. Discover means "to find something."

Find New Words Search through textbooks, magazines and newspapers to find three new words with the words *cover, new,* and *place*. Write them in your personal word journal. Also write the sentence in which you found each word. Then add these words to the Root Word Tree.

Be a Word Architect

discovery	newly	recovery	renew	replacement
irreplaceable	recover	rediscover	renewal	undiscovered

Directions Look at each branch of the tree below. Place each vocabulary word in the blank on the correct branch. Circle the common small word in each longer word.

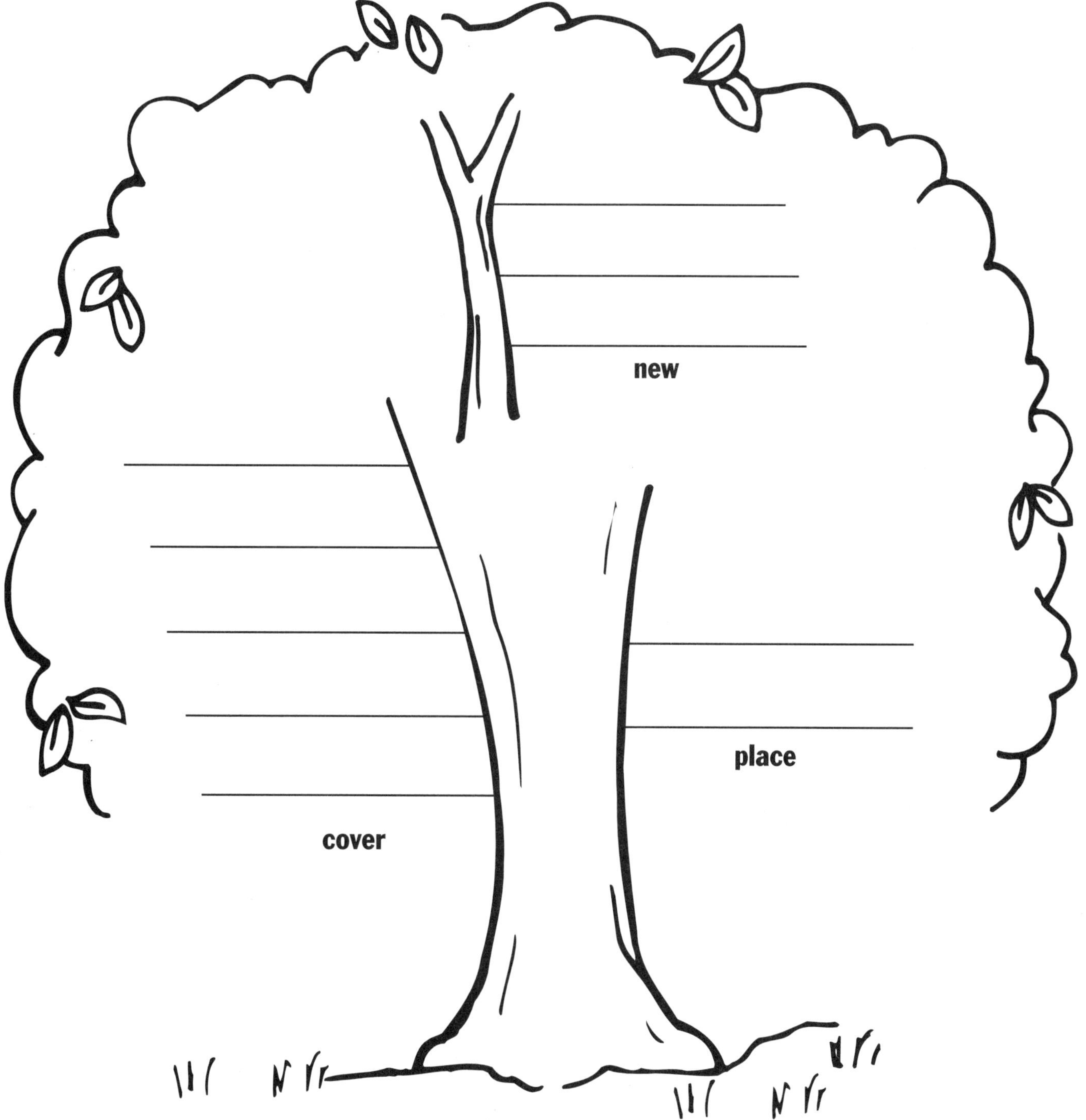

Connect Words and Meanings

discovery	newly	recovery	renew	replacement
irreplaceable	recover	rediscover	renewal	undiscovered

Directions Read each definition below. Then fill in the missing word to form the longer word that matches the definition. Write this word in the blank.

1. Definition: something that is found out or learned about for the first time

dis- + ______________________ + **-y** = ______________________

2. Definition: to make new, or as new, again; to begin again

re- + ______________________ = ______________________

3. Definition: not found; not known about

un- + **dis-** + ______________________ + **-ed** = ______________________

4. Definition: the act of putting back in place; something that takes the place of something else

re- + ______________________ + **-ment** = ______________________

5. Definition: very recently; lately

______________________ + **-ly** = ______________________

BONUS Write a sentence using two of the words above. ______________________________

____

(continued on next page)

Connect More Words and Meanings

discovery	newly	recovery	renew	replacement
irreplaceable	recover	rediscover	renewal	undiscovered

Directions Continue this activity. Read each definition below. Then fill in the missing word to form the longer word. Write this word in the blank.

6. Definition: to cover again; to get something back; to get better after being sick

re- + ______________________ = ______________________

7. Definition: not able to be replaced or something for which you can't put something else in its place

ir- + **re-** + ______________________ + **-able** = ______________________

8. Definition: the act of finding something that had been lost; coming back to health after sickness

re- + ______________________ + **-y** = ______________________

9. Definition: to find again

re- + **dis-** + ______________________ = ______________________

10. Definition: the act of making new or beginning again

re- + ______________________ + **-al** = ______________________

BONUS Write a sentence using two of the words above. ______________________________

____

Tell a Story Imagine that you discovered a treasure chest. Where was it? How did you find it? What was in it? Write a paragraph telling about your discovery. Try to make your story exciting and use at least three vocabulary words.

Learn Words in Context

discovery	**newly**	**recovery**	**renew**	**replacement**
irreplaceable	**recover**	**rediscover**	**renewal**	**undiscovered**

The Treasure at the Bottom of the Sea

Many years ago, a ship left the shores of Kadi. It was sailing to the island of Buru. It carried bright jewels, **newly** woven cloth, and shiny coins. Along the way, the sea became very rough. Heavy winds and huge waves hit the ship. The winds tore the sails and damaged other parts of the ship.

The captain and crew worked hard to save the ship. Luckily, nothing **irreplaceable** had been lost or destroyed. The crew repaired whatever they could. They put up another sail as a **replacement** for the one that had been torn. Because of their efforts, the boat was able to **recover** from the storm.

The seas were calm for a few days. Then, there was a sudden **renewal** of the stormy weather. The ship was at the mercy of the winds and waves again. This time, the ship was not able to make a **recovery**. It crashed onto rocks off the shore of Buru and sank.

It stayed at the bottom of the sea, **undiscovered** for many years. Then one day, a deep-sea diver was exploring the waters near Buru. She noticed part of an old ship sticking up from the sea bottom. She swam closer. She noticed other parts of the ship scattered about. She was very excited about her **discovery.** However, she was running out of oxygen. She came up to **renew** her air supply. Then she dove back down again. She wanted to **rediscover** the place where she had seen the sunken boat....

Use Words in Context

discovery	newly	recovery	renew	replacement
irreplaceable	recover	rediscover	renewal	undiscovered

Directions Write the correct word choice in the blank in each item.

1. The explorer had read about the ____________________ (*renewal, replacement, discovery*) of the ruins of an ancient city. Now he was searching the jungle for those ruins.

2. The lost city had lain ________________________ (*rediscovered, renewed, undiscovered*) for thousands of years because the jungle had covered it up.

3. The explorer was trying to find these ruins again. He wanted to ____________________ (*renew, rediscover, recovery*) them so that he could study them.

4. He was often tired. What he needed was the ______________________ (*newly, discovery, renewal*) of energy that only comes from a good night's sleep.

Directions Write an answer to each question in the blank. Be sure to use the boldface word in your answer.

5. What do you do to **recover** when you are sick?

____

6. Why should you take good care of something that is **irreplaceable**?

____

7. What would you do if a **newly** bought item did not work?

____

8. Where can you find a **replacement** for a broken bicycle seat?

____

Describe a Hidden Treasure Imagine you have something very valuable that can't be replaced. You decide to hide it. Write about this in your personal word journal. Describe what you are hiding and where. Use at least three vocabulary words.

Review and Extend

discovery	newly	recovery	renew	replacement
irreplaceable	recover	rediscover	renewal	undiscovered

Directions Build new words with *cover*, *new*, and *place*. Write the new word in the blank. Then write the letter of the definition that matches each new word in the blank by the number.

			NEW WORDS	DEFINITIONS
_____	**1.**	re- + **new** + -able =	____________	**A.** to take the cover off; to find
_____	**2.**	un- + **cover** =	____________	**B.** able to be made new or as new again
_____	**3.**	**new** + -ness =	____________	**C.** to put back in place
_____	**4.**	**place** + -ment =	____________	**D.** the act of putting something in a certain place
_____	**5.**	re- + **place** =	____________	**E.** quality of being new

Directions Fill in the blank in the following sentences with one of the new words you made in items 1–5.

6. It is time to ________________________ my old sneakers with a brand-new pair.

7. In time, the ____________________ of an unfamiliar place wears off. It becomes known.

8. You will have to ________________________ the pot to see if the water is boiling.

9. The two players argued over the ________________________ of the net.

10. The library books are ________________________ for two weeks.

"Cover" A "New" "Place" To prove that you have learned to add word parts together to understand long words, write one sentence that uses a word that contains *cover*, *new*, and *place* in that order. Your sentence must make sense. For example, you could write: "The *dis**cover**y* was a success because we found a ***new**ly* formed, *irre**place**able* underwater cave." You can also use words with *cover*, *new*, and *place* that are not on the list.

Check Your Mastery

Directions Read the items below. Write the word that fits in the blank.

1. Rita is in bed with the flu. She is resting so she will ______________________ (*renew, recover, rediscover*) soon.

2. That cup is very old. If it breaks, I cannot get another one like it. It is ______________________ (*renewal, irreplaceable, undiscovered*).

3. My library card has expired. I'll go to the library to ______________________ (*recover, rediscover, renew*) it.

4. Greg just painted his room green. He is proud of his ______________________ (*newly, irreplaceable, undiscovered*) painted room.

5. Max found a wallet and gave it back to the owner. He received a reward for the ______________________ (*discovery, recovery, renewal*) and return of the wallet.

6. The mayor said she wanted to make the old park beautiful again. She set aside money for the ______________________ (*replacement, renewal, discovery*) of the park.

7. The scientist tried to figure out how to make gold. Such a ______________________ (*recovery, renewal, discovery*) would make him very rich!

8. The secret passageway in the old castle was ______________________ (*irreplaceable, undiscovered, replacement*) for many years.

9. The light bulb in the hall burned out. Mr. Cherry had to put in a ______________________ (*replacement, recovery, renewal*).

10. The sailors found an island and drew a map showing how to get there. Then they lost the map. They were lucky to ______________________ (*recover, renew, rediscover*) the island.

Be a Word Architect

Vocabulary Words

armchair	**waterproof**
armload	**workforce**
soundproof	**workroom**
tabletop	**workshop**
waterfall	**worktable**

Word Learning Tip!

A compound word is made up of two words that are put together to make one new word. If you know the meaning of the words that make up a compound word, you can understand the meaning of the whole word.

Vocabulary Building Strategy

Use Compound Words
When you come across a compound word, look for the individual words that make it up. Then, think about what each individual word means. Next, add the meanings of the individual words together to see if you can come up with the meaning of the compound word. Finally, check to see if that meaning makes sense in the sentence in which you find the compound word.

Directions Read each compound word. Draw an up-and-down line between the two words that make up the compound word. Then write the two words in the blanks.

1. worktable __________ __________
2. tabletop __________ __________
3. workroom __________ __________
4. armchair __________ __________
5. workforce __________ __________
6. soundproof __________ __________
7. workshop __________ __________
8. waterfall __________ __________
9. armload __________ __________
10. waterproof __________ __________

Write About It If you had a workshop, what would you like to make or do in it? What tools or other things would you have in your workshop? Write a paragraph in your personal word journal. Use at least three vocabulary words.

Connect Words and Meanings

armchair	soundproof	waterfall	workforce	workshop
armload	tabletop	waterproof	workroom	worktable

Directions Each of the items below is a definition of a compound word. Put the two words in boldface together to make a compound word that fits the definition. Then write the word in the blank.

1. The **top** of a **table** is a ______________________________.

2. A stream of **water** that you see **fall** from a high place is a ______________________________.

3. A comfortable **chair** that lets you rest your **arms** is a(n) ______________________________.

4. A **room** where **work** is done is a ______________________________.

5. A **table** on which you can **work** with tools is a ______________________________.

(continued on next page)

Connect More Words and Meanings

armchair	soundproof	waterfall	workforce	workshop
armload	tabletop	waterproof	workroom	worktable

Directions Continue this activity. Put the two words in boldface together to make a compound word that fits the definition. Then write the word in the blank.

6. An amount or **load** that can be carried in one **arm** is a(n) ______________________ .

7. A group or **force** of people that do **work** is a ______________________ .

8. Something that can keep **water** out or is **proof** against water is ______________________ .

9. A room, shed, or **shop** where **work** such as making things or fixing things is done is a ______________________ .

10. Something that can keep **sound** out or is **proof** against sound is ______________________ .

Have a Matching Contest With a partner, make word cards for the following: *arm, chair, load, sound, proof, table, top, water, fall, work, force, room,* and *shop.* Shuffle the cards and place them face down. Take turns flipping cards over, two at a time. Give a point for every compound word formed. After all the cards are turned over, the person with the most points wins.

Learn Words in Context

armchair	soundproof	waterfall	workforce	workshop
armload	tabletop	waterproof	workroom	worktable

A Tall Tale

Benjo Bojo was a giant who liked to make things. He had a large **workroom** full of tools. Benjo Bojo was not only big, he was strong, too. When he worked, he could get as much done as a **workforce** of fifty people!

One day, he wanted to make a new **tabletop** for his kitchen table. He needed a lot of wood because his table was as big as a baseball field.

The giant walked into the forest and pulled up some trees with his bare hands. Then he picked up an **armload** of these trees and carried them back to his hut. He stacked the trees outside the **workshop** where he made things. He covered them with a huge **waterproof** cloth so that they wouldn't get wet if it rained.

The next day, Benjo Bojo sawed the wood. Some sawdust got into his nose, and he had to sneeze. It was so loud! You wouldn't have wanted to be anywhere near him, unless you were in a **soundproof** room and couldn't hear a thing!

All this work made Benjo Bojo hungry, so he made himself a snack. He ate a whole field of corn, and drank a whole **waterfall** of water! After that, Benjo Bojo felt tired. "I need a nice comfortable **armchair** to sit in," he said to himself. "Hmmm…what's big and soft that I can use?" He looked up into the sky and got an idea. He reached up and grabbed four fluffy clouds. He put the clouds on his **worktable** and tied them together. When he was finished, he put them on the floor, sat in his new chair, and took a nice, long nap.

Use Words in Context

armchair	soundproof	waterfall	workforce	workshop
armload	tabletop	waterproof	workroom	worktable

Directions In the blank after each item, write the vocabulary word that can replace the underlined phrase.

1. Hilda the grasshopper was so tired. She curled up in her comfortable sitting place and fell asleep for a hundred years. ______________________

2. Gabby the goldfish was a very good swimmer. She could swim up a stream tumbling over a high place. ______________________

3. Ozzie the octopus had eight long arms. He loved to wrap presents. He could wrap more than a group of hired workers! ______________________

4. Louis the lion has the loudest roar. You can hear him all over the forest, unless you are in a totally quiet place. ______________________

Directions Choose the correct vocabulary word to complete each sentence. Write the word in the blank.

5. A tent has to be ______________________ (*soundproof, armload, waterproof*) so campers can stay dry when it rains.

6. The glass table had a clear ______________________ (*tabletop, worktable, workroom*).

7. Jenna carried a(n) ______________________ (*workforce, armload, armchair*) of groceries up the stairs.

8. Gene put the wood on top of the ______________________ (*worktable, workshop, workforce*) where he had his hammer and saw.

Write Sentences About Folktale Characters In your personal word journal, write three sentences about animals doing impossible things. Use at least three vocabulary words.

Review and Extend

armchair	soundproof	waterfall	workforce	workshop
armload	tabletop	waterproof	workroom	worktable

Directions Use your knowledge of the compound words in this lesson to answer each question below. Write your answer on the line.

NEW WORDS **carload** **fireproof** **workstation**

1. Why is it important for a raincoat to be **waterproof?**

____

2. What is one thing you would expect to find on the **waterfront**?

____

3. Why would a drummer practice in a **soundproof** room?

____

4. Why should children's clothing be **fireproof**?

____

5. What is one thing you might find in a **workshop**?

____

6. Name one thing you might find at someone's **workstation** in addition to a computer?

____

7. If you were carrying an **armload** of firewood, would you be carrying about ten pieces of wood or one piece of wood?

____

8. If you had a **carload** of groceries, would you have about two bags or fifteen?

____

Create a Tall-Tale Character Imagine you are writing a tall tale. Who will the main character be? Write a paragraph describing this character. Use as many compound words as you can.

Check Your Mastery

Directions Write a word in the blank that shows you understand the meaning of the boldface word in each sentence.

1. An **armchair** is meant for ______________________________ .

2. On a kitchen **tabletop**, you might find a(n) ______________________________ .

3. You might carry an **armload** of ______________________________ to a fireplace.

4. In your **workshop** you might ______________________________ .

5. A **soundproof** room keeps out ______________________________ .

Directions Choose the correct vocabulary word to complete each sentence. Circle the correct word.

6. When the ________ goes home at night, the office building is empty.

   workroom **workforce** **tabletop**

7. Kevin likes to splash in puddles. It's a good thing his boots are ________ .

   waterfall **soundproof** **waterproof**

8. I saw a lot of cameras of all sizes in the photographer's ________ .

   workroom **workforce** **waterfall**

9. We hiked along the stream and had a picnic by the ________ .

   waterproof **workshop** **waterfall**

10. The artist's ________ was covered with pads of paper and colored pencils.

    workforce **armchair** **worktable**

Be a Word Architect

Directions Read each clue. Find a word in the box below that best fits. Write it in the blank. Then follow the directions below the clue to build a compound word.

down	walk	track	winder	spin
bar	up	splitting	lines	step

1. **Clue:** This is a straight stripe or band. ______________
2. Attach this word to the end of *side*.

   ____

3. **Clue:** This is what you take when you move your foot forward and bring it down. ________________________
4. Attach this word to the end of *side*. ________________

5. **Clue:** This word is the opposite of "up." ____________
6. Attach this word to the front of *side*. ________________

7. **Clue:** You do this when you travel by foot.

   ____

8. Attach this word to the end of *side*. ________________

9. **Clue:** These are long, thin marks you can make with a pen or pencil. ____________________
10. Attach this word to the end of *side*.

    ____

(continued on next page)

Vocabulary Words

downside	**sidestep**
sidebar	**sidetrack**
sidelines	**sidewalk**
sidespin	**sidewinder**
sidesplitting	**upside**

Word Learning Tip!

Some words are made up of two smaller words that are joined together. We call them compound words. If you know the meaning of the two smaller words, you can put those meanings together and understand the meaning of a bigger compound word. The meaning of a compound word is made up of the meaning of the two smaller words put together.

Vocabulary Building Strategy

Use Word Families Some words are related because they have the same smaller word in them. All of the vocabulary words in this lesson contain the word *side*. You can find the meaning of the new word by adding *side* to the meaning of the other word in the compound.

Be a Word Architect

downside	**sidelines**	**sidesplitting**	**sidetrack**	**sidewinder**
sidebar	**sidespin**	**sidestep**	**sidewalk**	**upside**

Directions Continue this activity. Read each clue. Find a word in the box that best fits. Write it in the blank. Then follow the directions below the clue to build a compound word.

down	**walk**	**track**	**winder**	**spin**
bar	**up**	**splitting**	**lines**	**step**

11. Clue: This is something that moves in twists and turns. ____________________

12. Attach this word to the end of *side*. ____________________

13. Clue: This word means "to turn around or twirl in a fast way." ____________________

14. Attach this to the end of *side*. ____________________

15. Clue: This word is the opposite of "down." ____________________

16. Attach this to the front of *side*. ____________________

17. Clue: This word means "to follow something or someone." ____________________

18. Attach this to the end of *side*. ____________________

19. Clue: This word means "bursting or breaking apart." ____________________

20. Attach this to the end of *side*. ____________________

Find New Compound Words Look through a book, newspaper, or magazine. Try to find at least three new words with *side* in them. Write the new compound words, along with their definitions, in your personal word journal.

Connect Words and Meanings

downside	sidelines	sidesplitting	sidetrack	sidewinder
sidebar	sidespin	sidestep	sidewalk	upside

Directions Read each definition below. Then complete the sentence in a way that shows you understand the definition.

1. **upside:** the top side; an advantage or good part of doing or having something

   The **upside** of having a pet is ______________________________

   ____

2. **downside:** the lower side; a disadvantage or drawback, not the good part; the opposite of *upside*

   The **downside** of having a pet is ______________________________

   ____

3. **sidewalk:** a paved path along the side of a street

   Before you step off the **sidewalk**, ______________________________

   ____

4. **sidespin:** a turning motion that spins a ball sideways

   A pitcher might put a **sidespin** on a ball to ______________________________

   ____

5. **sidelines:** the area outside the borders of the playing field; activities other than a person's regular job

   On the **sidelines**, the coach ______________________________

   ____

(continued on next page)

Connect More Words and Meanings

downside	sidelines	sidesplitting	sidetrack	sidewinder
sidebar	sidespin	sidestep	sidewalk	upside

Directions Continue this activity. Read each definition below. Then complete the sentence in a way that shows you understand the definition.

6. sidewinder: a small rattlesnake that moves in a sideways, looping motion

If I saw a **sidewinder**, I might ______________________________

____

7. sidebar: a short news story that is printed alongside a longer story. Often it appears in a long column that looks like a bar. Any information that is presented on the side of a printed page.

The news article about the campaign to clean up our school had a **sidebar** about

____

8. sidesplitting: extremely funny; so funny it makes you feel as though your sides will split from laughing so hard

I read a **sidesplitting** story about ______________________________

____

9. sidestep: to step to one side; to get out of the way; to avoid or get away from

The speaker tried to **sidestep** ______________________________

____

10. sidetrack: to move or distract someone from what he or she is doing; to turn aside from a main purpose or use

It's hard to keep my mind on my homework and not get **sidetracked** when

____

Write a Sidesplitting Joke What is the funniest joke you know? Write it on a piece of paper. Also tell why you find it so funny. Use at least two vocabulary words. Then tell the joke to your classmates and try to make them laugh.

Learn Words in Context

downside	sidelines	sidesplitting	sidetrack	sidewinder
sidebar	sidespin	sidestep	sidewalk	upside

A Telephone Conversation

Dina: Hi Jeff. What's new with you?

Jeff: You won't believe what happened on my way home! I saw a rattlesnake! I think it was a **sidewinder**, because it was moving sideways, in loops.

Dina: Where did you see it?

Jeff: I saw it on the **sidewalk**, in front of the house next door. I sure did a quick **sidestep** to get out of its way!

Dina: Well, the **upside** of that is now you have something exciting to tell everyone!"

Jeff: Yeah, sure…I can read all about it in the paper tomorrow. I can see it on the front page, in the **sidebar** with all the latest news. It will say: "Jeff Blaine saw a snake and lived to tell about it!"

Dina: So you'll be famous!

Jeff: But the **downside** is that I was really, really scared when I saw it!

Dina: That snake was probably more scared of you! Let's see, how much bigger are you?

Jeff: But I'm not poisonous! Hey, I don't want to **sidetrack** you, but can we talk about something else now? What have you been doing?

Dina: I just got home from the baseball game. I watched from the **sidelines** as our team won again! After the team won I was so happy, I jumped and did a **sidespin.** The game was very exciting at the end. The score was tied, 6 to 6. Jancy was at bat. The bases were loaded. Jancy hit a triple, and all of our players scored! Our team was so happy and we laughed so hard, it was **sidesplitting**!

Write a Sidebar Work with a partner. Brainstorm a short news feature about Jeff's snake episode. Then write a sidebar in your personal word journal. Try to use at least three vocabulary words and two new words that contain the word "side."

Use Words in Context

downside	sidelines	sidesplitting	sidetrack	sidewinder
sidebar	sidespin	sidestep	sidewalk	upside

Directions Answer each question. Use the word in boldface in your answer. Write your answer on the line.

1. Your cabin in the woods has no phone. What could be the **upside** of this?

____

2. What could be the **downside** of not having a telephone?

____

3. When doing homework, how can a friend's calling you on the phone **sidetrack** you?

____

4. Your friend tells you a **sidesplitting** joke. How do you react?

____

Directions Choose the word that best fits to complete each sentence. Write the word in the blank.

5. The small _______________ (*sidebar, sidewinder, sidestep*) moved quickly over the sand.

6. The car did a _______________ (*sidesplitting, sidetrack, sidespin*) when the other car hit it.

7. Kira swept the leaves off the _______________ (*sidewalk, sidelines, downside*) in front of her apartment building.

8. The _______________ (*upside, sidelines, sidebar*) in the newspaper told about a big windstorm.

9. There were many toys on the floor. Hal had to take a _______________ (*sidestep, downside, sidespin*) so he would not walk on one of them.

Write About Inventions Many inventions we use every day weren't around two hundred years ago. For example, people living then didn't have phones, electricity, airplanes, or computers. Choose one of these inventions. How has it made life easier? How has it made life more difficult? Write a paragraph about the upside or the downside of the invention. Use as many vocabulary words as you can.

Review and Extend

downside	sidelines	sidesplitting	sidetrack	sidewinder
sidebar	sidespin	sidestep	sidewalk	upside

Directions Choose the word from the box that answers the question. In the blanks, first write the second word that makes up the compound word. Then write the compound word.

NEW WORDS **sidecar** **sidedish** **sidesaddle** **sideshow** **sidewhiskers**

1. Cats have whiskers on the side of their faces. What might these be called?

side + ____________________ = ____________________

2. Onion rings are served on the side of a main dish. What might this dish be called?

side + ____________________ = ____________________

3. A motorcycle may have a small car attached to its side. What might this car be called?

side + ____________________ = ____________________

4. A saddle may be designed so that a person rides with both legs to one side. What do you think this type of saddle is called?

side + ____________________ = ____________________

5. If a circus has a small show on the side of its main tent, what might this show be called?

side + ____________________ = ____________________

6. **BONUS** Write a sentence using one vocabulary word and one new word.

____

Write About Your Favorite *Sidedish* Write a short description of your favorite *sidedish*. Then write a few sentences about when the dish is served and why you like it so much. Be sure to use the word *sidedish* in your description. You may also want to draw a picture of the sidedish.

Check Your Mastery

Directions Circle the letter of the best answer to each question.

1. Which of the following could be **sidesplitting**?

A. a serious news story
B. a very funny movie
C. a sad story
D. a mystery

2. Which of the following is a **sidewinder**?

A. a clock
B. a strong wind
C. a snake
D. a clock

3. Which of the following could be the **upside** of a heavy snowstorm?

A. stores having to close
B. dangerous roads
C. shoveling snow
D. going sledding

4. Who would NOT be on the **sidelines** of a soccer game?

A. people watching
B. the coaches
C. players waiting to play
D. players kicking the ball

5. What could be the **downside** of hot weather?

A. can go swimming
B. too hot to play ball
C. can play outside
D. can wear shorts and a t-shirt

Directions Choose the word that best completes each item. Write the word in the blank.

6. We like to roller-skate along the ______________________ (*sidebar, sidestep, sidewalk*).

7. Bob did not want his brother to ______________________ (*sidetrack, sidesplitting, sidespin*) him while he was trying to read so he asked him not to interrupt.

8. Each chapter in the textbook had a ______________________ (*sidetrack, sidebar, downside*) on the first page. It told the main points that would be covered.

9. The dancer twirled and then did a ______________________ (*sidelines, sidespin, upside*).

10. The marching band does a quick ______________________ (*sidestep, sidewinder, sidetrack*) where they move their feet to the left on the fourth beat.

Be a Word Architect

Learn More!

Learn More About Word Families

Knowing the meaning of the prefix and suffixes below will help you learn the meaning of the vocabulary words.

Prefix		Suffix	
a-	in the act of	**-er**	a person who
		-less	without; unable to
		-ness	state of or quality of (makes a noun)
		-y	like, feeling

Here's a spelling rule you should know. When a word ends in a consonant and *y*, change the *y* to *i* when you add a suffix that begins with a consonant.

sleepy + ness = sleepiness

Vocabulary Words

asleep	**sleepwalk**
sleepiness	**sleepwalker**
sleepless	**sleepwear**
sleeplessness	**sleepy**
sleepover	**sleepyhead**

Word Learning Tip!

Many words have a similar meaning because they contain the same main words. Words with the same main word can be grouped together and called a word family. They share a common word and all of their meanings are related. All of the words in this lesson contain the word *sleep*.

Vocabulary Building Strategy

Understand Word Families
If you know the meaning of the main word in a word family, it can help you learn the meaning of all the words in that family. All of the words in this lesson contain the word *sleep*. The related words can have a prefix, suffix, or another word attached to *sleep*. The word *sleep* means "to rest with eyes closed."

Be a Word Architect

asleep	sleepless	sleepover	sleepwalker	sleepy
sleepiness	sleeplessness	sleepwalk	sleepwear	sleepyhead

Directions Write each vocabulary word in the pillow that shows how it was made.

prefix + sleep

1. ______________________

sleep + suffix

2. ______________________
3. ______________________

sleep + suffix + suffix

4. ______________________
5. ______________________

sleep + word

6. ______________________
7. ______________________
8. ______________________

sleep + word + suffix

9. ______________________

sleep + suffix + word

10. ______________________

Write an Advertisement Find advertisements for beds and pillows. Circle the words it contains that tell about sleeping. In your personal word journal, copy the sentence in which you find each word. Then create an advertisement for a comfortable pillow or mattress. Use as many *sleep* words as you can.

Connect Words and Meanings

asleep	**sleepless**	**sleepover**	**sleepwalker**	**sleepy**
sleepiness	**sleeplessness**	**sleepwalk**	**sleepwear**	**sleepyhead**

Directions Read each definition below. Use your knowledge of word parts to choose the vocabulary word that best fits. Then use the vocabulary word to complete the sentence that follows the definition. Write the word in the blank. You may also use the glossary to help you.

1. **Definition:** not able to sleep ______________________

2. Jorge was ______________________ even though it was late. He read a book so he would get tired.

3. **Definition:** feeling like sleeping or ready to sleep; drowsy ______________________

4. As soon as Sitar felt ______________________ , she got ready to go to bed.

5. **Definition:** the state or condition of not being able to sleep ______________________

6. Some people count sheep to try to get over ______________________ .

7. **Definition:** in a state of sleep; sleeping ______________________

8. "Don't make a lot of noise! Louisa is still ______________________ !" said Cary.

9. **Definition:** the state or condition of being drowsy or ready to go to sleep

   ____

10. A good night's rest will take care of ______________________ .

(continued on next page)

Connect More Words and Meanings

asleep	sleepless	sleepover	sleepwalker	sleepy
sleepiness	sleeplessness	sleepwalk	sleepwear	sleepyhead

Directions Continue this activity. Read each definition below. Use your knowledge of word parts to choose the vocabulary word that best fits. Then use the vocabulary word to complete the sentence that follows the definition. Write the word in the blank. You may also use the glossary to help you.

11. Definition: clothing worn to sleep in ______________________________

12. Alisa's mother bought the pajamas in the ____________________ part of the store.

13. Definition: a person who feels tired and ready to go to sleep; a person whose head is filled with sleep and not ready to wake up ______________________________

14. Mother said, "Get up, my little ____________________, or you will be late for school."

15. Definition an event where one or more people sleep at another person's home

____

16. Mom let us order a pizza for the ______________________________.

17. Definition: to walk in your sleep ______________________________

18. Aunt Maura would sometimes ____________________ late at night. The next morning, she wouldn't remember being out of bed.

19. Definition: a person who walks in his or her sleep ______________________________

20. "Uncle Malachi was a ____________________, too," said Mom. "I would wake up in the middle of the night and see him walking down the hall."

Write About Sleep Signs Some people, particularly little children, try to pretend that they are not sleepy, even when they are. Work with your partner to brainstorm a list of signs of sleepiness. Then, in your personal word journal, write sentences explaining how you know someone is sleepy. For example, "I know my sister is sleepy when her eyes start to close." Try to use three "sleep" words in your sentences.

Learn Words in Context

asleep	**sleepless**	**sleepover**	**sleepwalker**	**sleepy**
sleepiness	**sleeplessness**	**sleepwalk**	**sleepwear**	**sleepyhead**

READ!

Lanie's Scary Party

Lanie was very excited. She had invited her favorite friends over for a **sleepover**. Carmen, Beth, and Kim were all going to spend the night at her house. First, they made popcorn. Then they watched a scary movie about a man who would **sleepwalk** every time the moon was full. While walking in his sleep, he became a monster. At day-break he would change back and never know what happened.

"That was a silly movie," said Kim afterwards. She didn't want anyone to know the movie had scared her.

"I agree," said Carmen. "Scary movies usually keep me up. This movie isn't going to make me **sleepless**, though. I'm going to sleep very well tonight."

"OK. So let's get ready for bed," said Lanie.

The girls changed their clothes, put on their **sleepwear,** and got into the bunkbeds. Lanie was about to turn the lights off.

"Wait!" said Beth, "It's not that I'm scared of the dark, but I'm not *really* **sleepy** yet. Can't we stay up and talk?"

"Yeah, let's stay up," Carmen quickly agreed.

"Hey, I have a great cure for **sleeplessness**!" said Lanie. "If you can't sleep, drink some warm milk. Next thing you know, you'll feel such **sleepiness**, you won't be able to keep your eyes open. You'll fall **asleep** in no time!"

"Yuk!" they all yelled.

Kim let out a big yawn and stretched out her arms.

"Oh, I think we have a **sleepyhead** among us now," Lanie remarked.

"Fine, as long as we don't have a **sleepwalker** among us!" Beth whispered to Carmen.

This made everybody laugh. They all felt better now.

Use Words in Context

asleep	sleepless	sleepover	sleepwalker	sleepy
sleepiness	sleeplessness	sleepwalk	sleepwear	sleepyhead

Directions Complete each sentence below. Write your answer in the blank.

1. If I'm not **sleepy** when I go to bed, I ______________________________ .
2. A fun activity to do at a **sleepover** is ______________________________ .
3. I usually fall **asleep** at night after ______________________________ .
4. If I saw a **sleepwalker**, I would ______________________________ .
5. My favorite piece of **sleepwear** is ______________________________ .
6. When I'm in bed but feel **sleepless**, I ______________________________ .
7. I would call someone a **sleepyhead** if ______________________________ .
8. I sometimes feel **sleeplessness** after ______________________________ .
9. If you **sleepwalk**, it can be dangerous because ______________________________ .
10. If **sleepiness** overcomes me while I'm watching a movie, I ______________________________

____ .

Draw a Word Web Write the word *sleepwear* in the center circle of a word web. What words do you think of when you think of *sleepwear*? Add these words to your word web.

Review and Extend

asleep	sleepless	sleepover	sleepwalker	sleepy
sleepiness	sleeplessness	sleepwalk	sleepwear	sleepyhead

Directions Read the new words and their definitions. Circle the word that best fits each sentence.

NEW WORDS

sleeper *noun* someone who sleeps

sleeplessly *adverb* in a way that shows you are not able to sleep

sleepier *adjective* more sleepy

sleepily *adverb* in a sleepy way

sleeping bag *noun* a padded bag in which you can sleep, often used for camping

1. Darin could not fall asleep. He tossed and turned ________________ in his bed.

   sleeper **sleeplessly** **sleepier**

2. Maxine felt much __________ after drinking a cup of warm chocolate.

   sleepier **sleeping bag** **sleeplessly**

3. Liz was in a deep sleep when the phone rang. She walked _______ to the phone.

   sleeper **sleepier** **sleepily**

4. Bart is a restless __________. He tosses and turns when he sleeps.

   sleeplessly **sleepier** **sleeper**

5. Alana lay in her ______ and looked up at the stars.

   sleepier **sleeplessly** **sleeping bag**

BONUS Write a sentence using one vocabulary word and one new word.

____

Repeat Tongue Twisters Tongue twisters are sentences with many words that start with the same sound. Work with a partner. Write a tongue twister using as many vocabulary and new words as you can from this lesson. Share your tongue twisters with other students. Challenge them to say it really fast three times and see what happens!

Check Your Mastery

Directions Choose the best word to complete each item. Write the word in the blank.

1. Sydney felt ____________________ (*sleeplessness, sleepy, sleepyhead*), so he went to bed.

2. Ben was so tired he fell ________________________ (*sleepover, sleepiness, asleep*) on the school bus.

3. Dylan used to _______________________ (*sleepwalk, sleepwalker, sleepyhead*). Now he sleeps soundly all night.

4. For her birthday, Nan got a new nightgown. Nan likes her new ____________________ (*sleepwear, sleepyhead, sleepiness*) very much.

5. Even though it was very late, Nick could not sleep. He was ________________________ (*sleepy, sleepless, sleepiness*) and wide awake.

Directions Circle the letter of the item that best completes each sentence below.

6. When **sleepiness** comes upon you, _______ .
   A. take a nap B. watch a movie C. call a friend

7. Something you might do at a **sleepover** is _______ .
   A. swim in the ocean B. go to school C. tell stories

8. You might see a **sleepwalker** _______ .
   A. buying groceries B. riding a horse C. strolling down the hall

9. What a **sleepyhead** wants most is _______ .
   A. to get up B. to hear a story C. more sleep

10. After a night of **sleeplessness**, a person probably feels _______ .
    A. rested B. tired C. happy

Chapter 3

Content Words

Learn Words About a New Subject

Vocabulary Words

hexagon **rectangle**
octagon **triangle**
pentagon

Word Learning Tip!

When you read about a new subject, you see new content words. They are not the words that you read in most other books. Content words may be the longest and most difficult words in the text. Usually, they appear many times. A clue to their meanings is that they give you special information about the topic you are studying. For example, all content words in this lesson tell something about types of geometric shapes and figures.

Vocabulary Building Strategy

To learn the meaning of a new content word, think about how it relates to the main subject of the text you are reading. The new word will tell something specific about that big idea or subject. For example, in this lesson, you know that all the content words relate to shapes or figures. Use this big idea to determine the exact meaning of each content word.

Directions Look at the storyboard below. Think about how the boldface words are connected to the topic. They work together to give you information about shapes.

Mr. Dobson's class learned about five different geometric shapes. Then the class went on a scavenger hunt to find items that looked like these figures.

On the corner, Charmaine saw a STOP sign. "I found an **octagon**," she said. "The STOP sign has eight angles and eight sides."

Charmaine saw a boy wearing a t-shirt. "Here's my **hexagon**," she thought. "Just look at his t-shirt. It has a symbol inside a figure with six sides and six angles. This is the Chinese symbol for joy."

Learn Words About a New Subject

Charmaine stopped at a new bookstore. "The store sign is a **rectangle**," she said. "It has four angles and four sides. Each flag looks like a **triangle**, which has three angles and three sides."

Charmaine needed to find one more geometric shape. She saw a school crossing sign. She counted the angles and sides. "This sign is a **pentagon**. It has five angles and five sides," Charmaine thought happily.

Connect Words and Meanings

hexagon **octagon** **pentagon** **rectangle** **triangle**

Directions Complete the crossword puzzle. Each clue is about a vocabulary word. You may use the glossary to help you.

Across

1. the number of sides and angles that a rectangle has
2. the number of sides and angles that a triangle has
3. the number of sides and angles that a hexagon has
5. a figure with four sides and four angles
7. a figure with five sides and five angles
8. the number of sides and angles that an octagon has

Down

1. the number of sides and angles that a pentagon has
2. a figure with three sides and three angles
4. a figure with six sides and six angles
6. a figure with eight sides and eight angles

Understand How Content Words Relate All the content words come from Greek and Latin, two ancient languages. The word *triangle* means "three (tri-) angles." The word *rectangle* means "right (rectus) angle." The prefix *penta* means "five," *hexa-* means "six", *octa-* means "eight," and *-gon* means "angle." Each content word tells how many angles and sides a shape has. In your personal journal, make a drawing beside each content word that shows how many angles and sides each word has.

Use Content Words

hexagon **octagon** **pentagon** **rectangle** **triangle**

Directions Look at the figures below. They are labeled A, B, C, and D. Use the vocabulary words to answer each question.

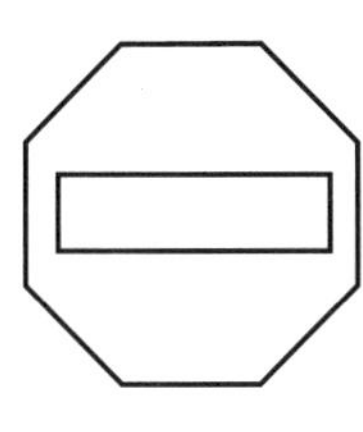
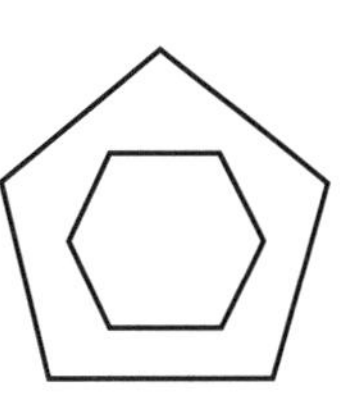
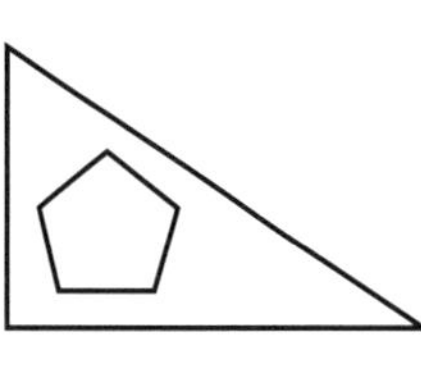

A **B** **C** **D**

1. In A, which figure is around the triangle? ____________________

2. In B, which figure is around the rectangle? ____________________

3. In C, which figure is inside the pentagon? ____________________

4. In D, which figure is inside the triangle? ____________________

5. Which has the fewest number of sides:
a hexagon, octagon, or triangle? ____________________

6. Look at pictures A, B, C, and D.
Which two pictures contain a triangle? ____________________

7. Which two pictures contain a rectangle? ____________________

8. Which two pictures contain a pentagon? ____________________

Why We Use Shape Patterns Work with a partner. List as many objects as you can that are shaped like the content words in this lesson. After each word, make a drawing and tell why you think that shape is well-suited for that object.

Put Words Into Action

hexagon **octagon** **pentagon** **rectangle** **triangle**

Directions Study the architect's sketch at right for a new elementary school. Then write the correct vocabulary words in the instructions that the architect wrote.

Nunoz Elementary School

Preschool classrooms

Kindergarten classrooms

Gym

Classrooms for Grades 1-2

Classrooms for Grades 3-6

Offices

Entrance

Entrance

1. The building for the Grades 3–6 classrooms is longer than it is wide. It is in the shape of a(n) ________________ .

2. The offices for the principal and teachers are in a special building. It is in the shape of a(n) ________________ .

3. The building for Grades 1–2 is on the left side. It is in the shape of a(n) ________________ .

4. Kindergarten students have their own building. It forms the figure called a(n) ________________ .

5. The preschool classrooms are behind the kindergarten classrooms. This building is shaped like a(n) ________________ .

6. The school has a gym building. It is shaped like a(n) ________________ .

7. The building that is shaped like a(n) ________________ has the most number of sides.

8. The building that is shaped like a(n) ________________ has the fewest sides.

Design Your Own Building Draw a building for the future. Try to use all the figures in this lesson as well as other shapes. Use the content words to write a paragraph that describes how your building will look and be used.

Review and Extend

hexagon **octagon** **pentagon** **rectangle** **triangle**

BONUS WORDS Here are two new words about shapes. Remember that these words deal with the same idea as your vocabulary words. That means that even if you have never seen these words before, you know something important about them—they tell about geometric shapes.

flat figure a figure that has only two dimensions—length and width

polygon a flat figure with three or more sides and angles

Directions Read each item. Choose the vocabulary word or the new bonus word that best fits the context. Write the word in the blank.

1. Ms. Amato asked each child to draw a different ________________, or flat figure. They could use these different shapes to make boards for games.

2. Hiang used chalk to draw a large ________________. Then she drew a circle at each of its five angles.

3. Valery wanted to play hopscotch. She drew one long ________________ with four sides. Then she added another one that crossed over at the top to form a "T."

4. Ray drew a game board for eight different players. Each player would start at a different corner. This game board had the shape of a(n) ________________.

5. Deena amazed everyone. She made a(n) ________________ by putting six triangles together.

6. "I'm very pleased," exclaimed Ms. Amato. "Today you made polygons, or ________________ with only two dimensions. Tomorrow you will make figures with three dimensions."

Learn New Content Words Related to Shapes Think of as many new content words about shapes as you can. List each one you identify. Beside it, sketch what it looks like. To help you get started, here's a content word that names a shape: *square*. Use the Word Learning Tip and Vocabulary Building Strategy to learn new words.

Check Your Mastery

Directions Read each item below. Write the vocabulary word that best fits in each sentence.

1. Each crossing guard got an eight-sided badge that was shaped like a(n) ____________________ .

octagon **hexagon** **triangle**

2. Amy played a musical instrument that has three sides. It gets its name from its shape, which is a ____________________ .

triangle **pentagon** **hexagon**

3. The architect drew a four-sided figure to show where the swimming pool would go. This figure is a ____________________ .

hexagon **rectangle** **triangle**

4. Andy is doing a crossword puzzle. He needs a word for a polygon that has six sides. He needs the word ____________________ .

pentagon **octagon** **hexagon**

5. Lisa is making an origami figure. She folds a piece of paper so that it has five angles and five sides. It is a ____________________ .

rectangle **hexagon** **pentagon**

Directions Write the letter of each polygon in the blank by its correct name.

_____ **6.** hexagon **A.**

_____ **7.** pentagon **B.**

_____ **8.** triangle **C.**

_____ **9.** rectangle **D.**

_____ **10.** octagon **E.**

Learn Words About a New Subject

Directions Look at the animal postcards below and on the next page. Think about how the boldface words are connected to the topic as you read each card. Together, the cards and words will give you information about places where people and animals live.

Each of the animals on the cards lives in a different **habitat**. There are many different kinds of **habitats** in which animals can live.

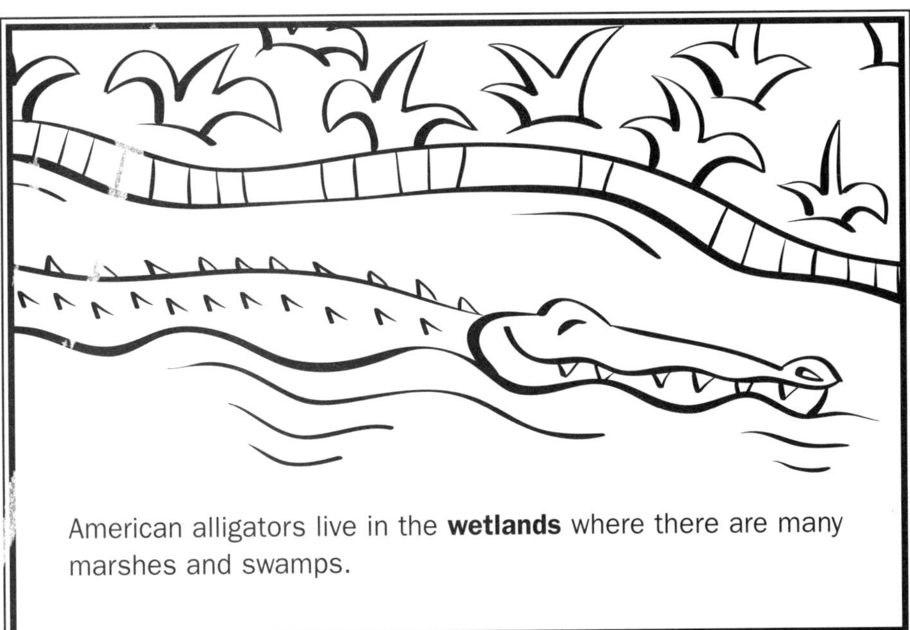

American alligators live in the **wetlands** where there are many marshes and swamps.

Vocabulary Words

desert	**habitat**
environment	**wetlands**
grasslands	

Word Learning Tip!

When you read about a new subject, you may see words you have not seen before in your everyday reading. These words are often the longest and most difficult in the text. They tell something specific about the subject you are reading. To learn these unknown words, think about the main idea, or subject. In this lesson, all the words tell about places where people and animals live.

Vocabulary Building Strategy

To learn the meaning of content words that tell about a new subject, make connections between the unfamiliar words and the main idea, or subject. The new word will tell something specific about that big (main) idea or subject. Tie the big idea and the meanings of other content words in the text together to learn the exact meaning of an unknown content word.

Learn Words About a New Subject

desert **environment** **grasslands** **habitat** **wetlands**

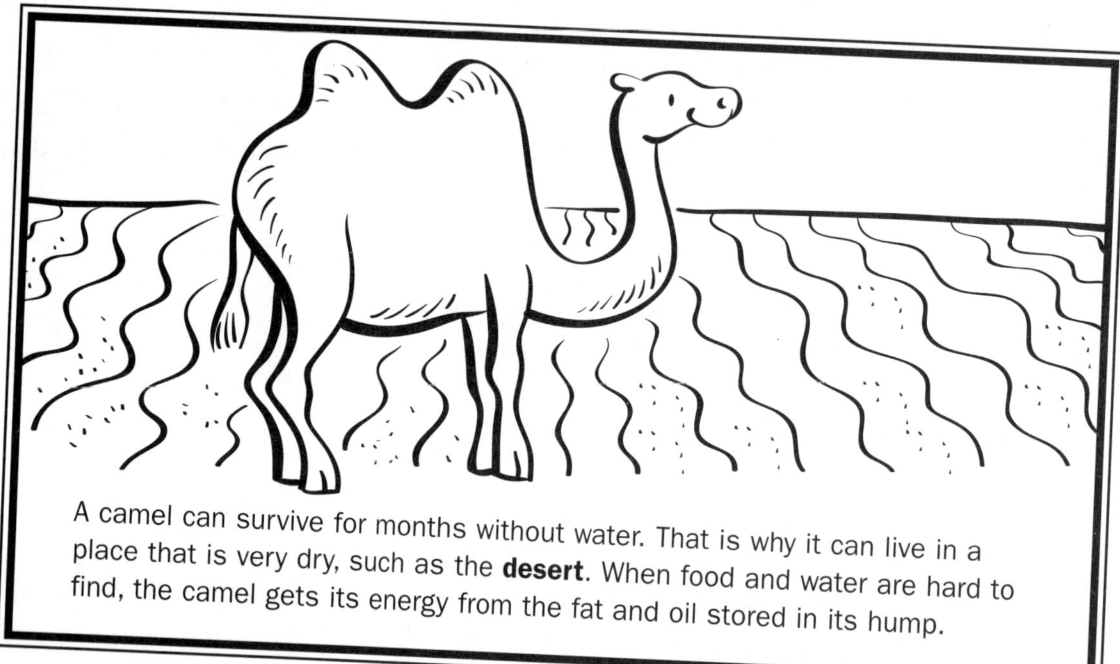

A camel can survive for months without water. That is why it can live in a place that is very dry, such as the **desert**. When food and water are hard to find, the camel gets its energy from the fat and oil stored in its hump.

Buffalo once roamed American **grasslands** by the millions.

Everything in the natural world—the land, the sea, the air—makes up our **environment**. All living things live in certain **habitats** within the **environment**. For example, a buffalo needs a lot of grass to eat. It could not live in a **desert** where the air is dry and the land is without much grass or water. Its habitat is the **grasslands**.

Connect Words and Meanings

desert	environment	grasslands	habitat	wetlands

Directions Read each definition below. Write the word that fits the definition on the first blank. Then write this word in the blank to complete the second sentence. You may use a dictionary or the glossary to help you.

1. **Definition:** land where there is a lot moisture in the soil, such as marshes and swamps ____________________
2. ____________________ are important because they provide homes to animals such as beavers, cranes, and ducks.
3. **Definition:** large, open areas of grass, such as pasture or prairie ____________________
4. Prairie dogs who live in the ____________________ eat all the grass around their burrows so that they can see far away.
5. **Definition:** the natural home of a group of plants and animals ____________________
6. The ocean is the natural ____________________ for fish and whales.
7. **Definition:** all of the natural world of land, sea, and air ____________________
8. It is important to protect our ____________________ so that people in the future will have clean air and water.
9. **Definition:** dry, often sandy land that gets very little rain ____________________
10. You can find different types of cactuses growing in the ____________________ .

Write About a Habitat In your personal journal, write about a habitat that is common where you live, such as wetlands, a forest, or a desert. First find information about the habitat. Then describe the animals and plants that live there. Use two content words and three other science words that describe this habitat. Use the Word Learning Tip and Vocabulary Building Strategy as you read about your habitat to learn three new science words.

Use Content Words

desert **environment** **grasslands** **habitat** **wetlands**

Directions Read the information about each habitat. Write the correct vocabulary word in each blank.

There are many different habitats in our (**1**) ______________________ . A special (**2**) ______________________ can be a desert, grassland, or wetland.

A (**3**) ______________________ habitat is very dry and gets very little rainfall. It can be very hot during the day and very cold at night. Because there is little rainfall, many plants that live in the (**4**) ______________________ store water. Animals that live in this special (**5**) ______________________ are usually smaller, such as jackrabbits and elf owls.

A (**6**) ______________________ habitat is very grassy, with few trees and shrubs. It can get very windy on the grasslands. Many different kinds of animals live in this (**7**) ______________________ , from large animals such as antelopes and buffalo to smaller animals such as prairie dogs, to small insects such as grasshoppers and beetles.

A (**8**) ______________________ habitat is covered with water for part or even all of the year. Some animals, such as fish and crabs, live in the water. Other animals, such as frogs, turtles, and birds live near the water. Swamps and marshes make up part of this special (**9**) ______________________ .

Animals and plants depend on their habitats for staying healthy. It is important that we protect our (**10**) ______________________ , the oceans, the land, and the air, so that they will survive.

Discuss the Environment In small groups, discuss why taking care of the environment is important for animals and people. What are some events or actions that endanger the environment? Write three sentences to describe what your group wants people to do to protect the environment. Underline the vocabulary words that you use.

Put Words Into Action

desert **environment** **grasslands** **habitat** **wetlands**

Directions Read each clue. Then write the vocabulary word that answers the question "What am I?"

1. Horses and deer can graze on my grass. What am I? ______________________

2. Ducks and geese live in my ponds and rivers. What am I? ______________________

3. There are many different kinds of me. Each special type is home to many different plants and animals. What am I? ______________________

4. You can see different kinds of plants and animals that don't need much water living in my soil. What am I? ______________________

5. People who care about me fight pollution of the earth. What am I? ______________________

6. I like air that is very dry. I don't like rain at all. Some animals that like me are camels and lizards. What am I? ______________________

7. I am the land, the air, and the sea. I am everything around you. What am I?

____

8. I like land where there is a lot of water. Some words that describe me are damp, moist, and humid. What am I? ______________________

9. I am the special place and natural conditions where certain animals and plants live. What am I? ______________________

10. I am a place where there is a lot of grass. In fact, I am known for my beautiful prairies with a lot of wildflowers. What am I? ______________________

Choose a Habitat In your personal word journal, write a paragraph that includes several new environment content words. First, choose a habitat. Use at least two vocabulary words along with the new science words you found that tell something specific about this habitat. If possible, go online or go through a science book to find these words.

Review and Extend

desert **environment** **grasslands** **habitat** **wetlands**

BONUS WORDS Here are three new words that relate to places where people and animals live, and what they have to do to live there. Even if you have never seen these words before, remember that these words all deal with the same main idea as your vocabulary words, places where people and animals live.

tundra a cold region, such as parts of Alaska, where there are no trees and the soil under the surface of the earth is always frozen

adapt to change and adjust to certain conditions

survive to continue to live or exist; to stay alive through or after a dangerous event

Directions Read each item below. Choose the vocabulary word or a new bonus word that best fits the context. Write it in the blank.

1. Land, sea, air, plants, and animals are all part of the ______________________ .

2. Animals often ______________________ , or adjust, in order to live in a place.

3. During the day it can be very hot and sunny in the ______________________ . Some animals that live here move at night looking for food.

4. It is hard to ______________________ in a cold climate during winter months when there is little food to eat. Some animals hibernate, or sleep, when it starts to get too cold. Other animals migrate, or travel, to warmer regions.

5. The plants in the ______________________ get dry during hot months. Lightning sets fire to the grasses. Animals that live here have to be able to run fast to escape the fires.

6. In the ______________________ regions of Alaska, it gets very cold in the winter.

Research an Animal Discuss how animals adapt to their habitats to survive. For example, how would a bear have to change to live in the desert? How could a hippo live in the grasslands? Have each person in your group choose an animal to research and tell how it has adapted to live in its habitat. Write about it in your personal word journal. Use three new content words you learned.

Check Your Mastery

Direction Read each item below. Circle the letter of the vocabulary word that best fits in each sentence.

1. Many animals live in the swampy ____ .

A. desert **B.** wetlands **C.** grasslands

2. If you are a rancher and have land for your cows to graze on, your ranch would be in a ____ area.

A. desert **B.** environment **C.** grasslands

3. When traveling across the ____ it is important to carry a supply of water.

A. desert **B.** habitat **C.** grasslands

4. The park ranger oversees a forest ____ .

A. grasslands **B.** wetlands **C.** habitat

5. It's important to take care of the ____ because we all need clean air, water, and land to live.

A. environment **B.** habitat **C.** grasslands

Directions Read the passage about snakes. Write the correct vocabulary word in each blank.

Snakes make up the largest group of reptiles. There are over 2,000 different species living in a variety of different (**6**) ________________ (s) all over the world. The diamondback rattlesnake lives in the dry (**7**) ________________ . It is common to the Southwest United States. The anaconda, the biggest snake in the world, lives in the (**8**) ________________ . It is found in the swamps in South America. The fiercest snake is a poisonous snake that lives in the forest and (**9**) ________________ of central Australia. Be sure to stay away from this snake. It is very poisonous and has a deadly bite. There are some snakes that do not have to live in one special place. They can be found almost everywhere throughout the (**10**) ________________ . For example, you can find the common garter snake in forests, fields, and ponds.

Learn Words About a New Subject

Vocabulary Words

comet **planet**
galaxy **universe**
orbit

Word Learning Tip!

When you read about a new subject, you may see words you have not seen before in your everyday reading. These words are often the longest and most difficult in the text. They tell you something specific about the topic. To learn these new words, think about the big idea or subject. In this lesson, all the words tell about space.

Vocabulary Building Strategy

To learn the meaning of content words that tell about a new subject, make connections between the unknown word and the big idea or subject. The new word will tell something specific about that big idea or subject. Tie together the big idea and the meaning of other content words that you know in the text. This will help you learn the exact meaning of the unknown content words.

Directions Look at the scenes below. Think about how the words in boldface type are connected to the topic as you look at each picture. The words and pictures will give you information about space.

"This is Earth. It is the **planet** on which we live. Earth is one of nine **planets**, or heavenly bodies, that circle, or **orbit** the sun. It takes the earth one year to make one **orbit** around the sun."

Learn Words About a New Subject

comet	galaxy	orbit	planet	universe

"Besides the nine **planets**, there are smaller objects that go around the sun. For example, a **comet** travels around the sun. A **comet** is made up of gas, ice, and dust. It is like a big, dirty snowball. It has a long tail of light."

The sun is a star. It is one of many stars in the **galaxy** in which people on Earth live. Our **galaxy** is called the Milky Way **Galaxy**. It is made up of over 100 billion stars."

Connect Words and Meanings

comet **galaxy** **orbit** **planet** **universe**

Directions Read each word. Match it to the correct definition. Write the letter of the definition by the word it defines. You may use a dictionary or the glossary to help you.

1. ______ orbit

2. ______ comet

3. ______ galaxy

4. ______ planet

5. ______ universe

A. everything that exists in space

B. a large group of stars and planets

C. one of nine heavenly bodies that circle the sun

D. to travel in a circle around a planet or the sun

E. a bright object made up of ice, gas, and dust with a long tail of light

Directions Read each clue. Then complete the sentence with the correct vocabulary word. Write the word in the blank.

6. I am made of dust and gas and have a very long tail. I travel around the sun. Scientists think there are millions of me in space. I am a ______________________ .

7. Earth, Venus, and Mars are heavenly bodies that orbit the sun. We are ______________ (s).

8. I am a huge group of stars and planets. I am a ______________________ .

9. Planets circle the sun in the same direction. The word for this is ______________ .

10. I am everything in all of space. I am bigger than anyone can ever imagine. I am the ______________ .

Learn Words Related to Space The word *galaxy* comes from the Greek word for "milk." Our galaxy is called the "Milky Way." Find information about the Milky Way in a book or on the Internet. In your personal word journal, tell how a galaxy might look like milk. Use at least three vocabulary words and two new content words in your description.

Use Content Words

comet **galaxy** **orbit** **planet** **universe**

Directions Use the vocabulary words to complete each sentence. Write the word in each blank.

1. The long tail of a ______________________ can be in the front or back of its body, but it always points away from the sun.

2. Jupiter and Saturn are the two biggest ______________________ (s) in our galaxy.

3. Uranus ______________________ (s) the sun a bit differently than other planets. It spins on its side when it moves around the sun.

4. The ______________________ where we live has nine planets and billions of stars.

5. There are billions more galaxies beyond our own galaxy. In fact, scientists have discovered in recent years that the ________________ is getting bigger and bigger.

Directions Write the correct vocabulary word to label each part of this diagram.

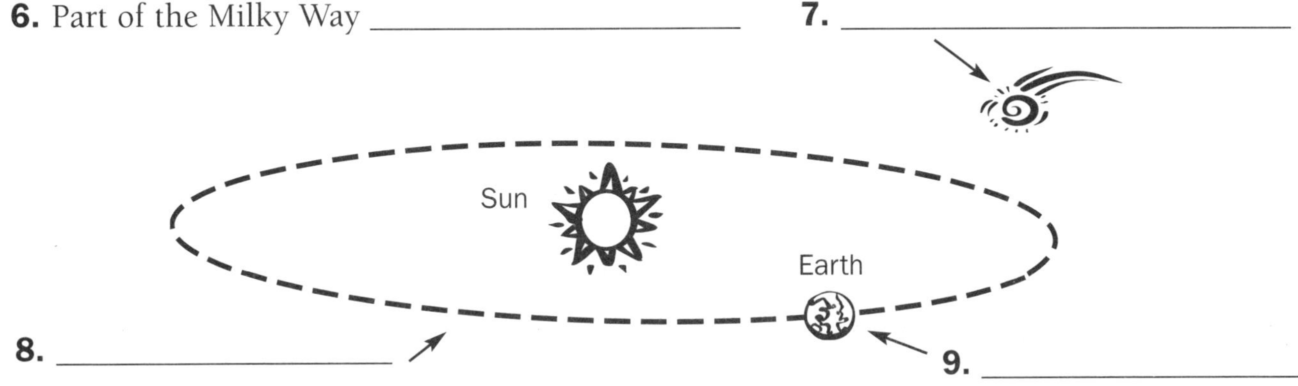

10. The ______________________ is made up of many planets, stars, and other objects.

Write a Space Message Work with a partner to write a message to put in a spacecraft that is going to Mars. Brainstorm what you want to say about the world in which you live. Write the message on a separate piece of paper. Use all the vocabulary words along with two more new space words. Use the Word Learning Tip and Vocabulary Building Strategy to learn the meaning of the new content words.

Put Words Into Action

comet **galaxy** **orbit** **planet** **universe**

Directions Read each fact and then choose the vocabulary word that best completes it. Write it in the blank.

1. Many scientists believe that billions of years ago the ______________________ (*universe, orbit*) was a huge ball that exploded in a big bang.

2. Earth and Venus are ______________ (s) (*galaxy, planet*) that are about the same size.

3. Saturn has 18 moons, the most moons of any planet in our ______________________ (*planet, galaxy*). Mercury and Venus do not have any moons.

4. In 1995, a very large and bright ________________ (*universe, comet*) was discovered by Alan Hale in New Mexico and Thomas Bopp in Arizona.

5. In the 1970s, two Voyager spacecrafts discovered three new moons that ____________ (*planet, orbit*) Jupiter and a ring that is 20 miles thick!

Directions Use the above facts to answer the questions. Use a vocabulary word in each answer.

6. Which two people discovered a very large and bright **comet**?

____

7. Which two **planets** are about the same size?

____

8. How do many scientists think the **universe** started?

____

Prove You Can Learn Content Words Read about a science subject that interests you. As you read, use the Word Learning Tip and Vocabulary Building Strategy to learn three new content words about that subject. Write a paragraph describing how you learned these words.

Review and Extend

comet **galaxy** **orbit** **planet** **universe**

BONUS WORDS Here are three new words that relate to space. Remember that these words all deal with the same big idea as your vocabulary words. This means that even if you have never seen these words before, you know one important fact—they all tell you something about space.

lunar having to do with the moon

solar system the sun and the bodies that move in orbit around it

telescope an instrument that makes faraway objects seem closer and larger, used to study planets, stars and other objects

Directions Read the article below. Write the correct vocabulary word or new bonus word in each blank.

The distances between planets and other heavenly bodies in our (**1**) ____________________ (*planet, galaxy, orbit*) are very great. For example, the moon is 240,000 miles from Earth. It took a spacecraft two days to travel to the moon and land on the (**2**) ____________________ (*universe, telescope, lunar*) landscape. The moon makes one (**3**) ____________________ (*lunar, orbit, comet*) around the Earth every 28 days.

It took Voyager 2 twelve years to reach Neptune. It is the only spacecraft to visit this (**4**) ____________________ (*solar system, planet, comet*). Neptune is a planet in our (**5**) ____________________ (*solar system, planet, lunar*). It is called an outer planet because it is 2,701 million miles from Earth. It will take a long time before people set foot on the outer planets, but there is another way to find out about them.

Scientists can look through a (**6**) ____________________ (*planet, telescope, solar system*) at these planets that are far away. Telescopes are so powerful today that scientists could look very closely at the amazing tails of light on the last (**7**) ____________________ (*comet, planet, lunar*) that was seen from Earth. Scientists are even using radio telescopes that use sound to find out more exciting information about our (**8**) ____________________ (*orbit, universe, telescope*).

Plan to Travel to Another Planet or Place Write about a planet or place that you and a partner are interested in traveling to in the future. Find out more about this planet or place. Use the Word Learning Tip and Vocabulary Building Strategy to learn three new content words. Be prepared to teach the class the new words and how you learned them.

Check Your Mastery

Directions Read each item below. Circle the letter of the word that best fits in each sentence.

1. Like the planet Earth, Saturn and Neptune _________ around the sun.

A. orbit **B.** universe **C.** galaxy

2. Mercury is the closest _________ to the sun. Pluto, Uranus and Neptune are farthest away from the sun.

A. universe **B.** orbit **C.** planet

3. Our _________, the large group of planets and stars where we live, is called the Milky Way.

A. comet **B.** galaxy **C.** planet

4. A _________ has a head that is filled with a lot of water, dust and gas and a very, very long tail.

A. universe **B.** orbit **C.** comet

5. The _________ has many other galaxies besides the Milky Way, and scientists who study outer space want to learn more about them.

A. galaxy **B.** universe **C.** comet

Directions Read the passage about the solar system. Write the correct vocabulary word in each blank.

Our solar system is made up of stars, moons, a sun and nine (**6**) ____________________(s). These planets circle, or (**7**) ____________________the sun. There are smaller objects, such as moons, small rocks, and (**8**) ____________________(s) with heads and tails that are also part of this system. Our solar system is a small part of the Milky Way (**9**) ____________________. All of these planets, moons, small rocks, and comets are what make the (**10**) ______________________________so interesting to study and learn more about.

Learn Words About a New Subject

Directions As you look at the scenes below, think about what you know about coming to a new land. How are the boldface words connected to this topic? Each word tells you something specific about this big idea.

Many people come to the United States every year. A person who comes to a new country to live is a **newcomer.** Today, people travel mostly in buses, cars, trains, and airplanes to get here.

Vocabulary Words

ancestor **newcomer**
contribution **tradition**
culture

Word Learning Tip!

When you read about a new subject, you may see new words that you have not seen before in your everyday reading. These words may be the longest and most difficult words in the text. They tell you something specific about the subject. To learn these new words, think about the big idea or subject about which you are reading. In this lesson, all of the words tell about coming to a new land.

Vocabulary Building Strategy

To learn the meaning of content words that tell about a new subject, make connections between the unknown word and the big idea. The new word will tell something specific about that big idea. Tie together the big idea and the meanings of other content words that you know in the text. This will help you to determine the exact meaning of the unknown content words.

Learn Words About a New Subject

Newcomers make many **contributions** to this country. They bring with them their own **traditions**, or customs, such as celebrations that are special to them and favorite recipes for food that they like to eat. Sometimes these **traditions** go back to **ancestors** who lived hundreds of years ago.

Culture is made up of the arts, beliefs, and customs of a people. American music, books, and art have been created by many different people coming from countries all over the world as well as by the Native Americans who were already here. They have all made **contributions** to American **culture**.

Connect Words and Meanings

ancestor **contribution** **culture** **newcomer** **tradition**

Directions Fill in the crossword puzzle. Each clue relates to a vocabulary word or a word that is part of a definition. You may use a dictionary or the glossary to help you.

Across

3. One of your ancestors is your great ______ -grandfather.
4. the arts, beliefs, and customs of a group of people
6. Beliefs and _______ (s) are part of a tradition.
7. ______ and music are part of the culture of a country.
9. something that is given

Down

1. a member of a family who lived a long time ago
2. someone who has come to a new place
5. something passed down, especially a custom, idea, or belief
8. A newcomer is a person who has just arrived in a new _______.

1 2 3 4 5 6 7 8 9

Tell a Story Faith Ringgold is an American artist who creates "Tell Stories" quilts about her life. Work with a partner and talk about a family tradition. It can be from your family or the family in a movie or television show. Then write about it in your journal. Include at least four vocabulary words and two new content words.

Use Content Words

ancestor **contribution** **culture** **newcomer** **tradition**

Directions Read the article. Use content words to complete each item. Write the vocabulary word that best fits in the blank.

On May 5 many people like to celebrate Cinco de Mayo. This means Fifth of May. The holiday honors an important battle in Mexico in 1862. The soldiers who fought in this battle made a great (**1**) ________________ (*culture, ancestor, contribution*) to Mexico. Cinco de Mayo truly marked the beginning of Mexico's independence.

The celebration is filled with (**2**) ________________ (s) (*tradition, culture, ancestor*) that have been passed down. There's a big parade with colorful costumes, banners, and flowers. Bands play Mexican songs. People dance. And there is traditional food.

Celebrating this holiday can make (**3**) ________________ (s) (*contribution, newcomer, culture*) feel welcome. It reminds them of the places where they were born and of (**4**) ________________(s) (*tradition, ancestor, newcomer*) who lived long ago. Mexican Americans have made an important (**5**) ________________ (*tradition, contribution, newcomer*) to the United States by sharing this holiday with all Americans.

There are also other (**6**) ________________ (s) (*ancestor, tradition, newcomer*) that people have passed down from their (**7**) ________________ (s) (*culture, contribution, ancestor*). There are Chinese New Year parades and West Indian Carnivals. Today, people from all over the world who come to the United States still contribute dance, art, and music to American (**8**) ________________ (*culture, ancestor, contribution*).

Create a Holiday Celebration Read about celebrations. Brainstorm an idea for one. What event will you celebrate? What costumes will people wear? What food will people eat? Will there be music? Write your description. Use at least three vocabulary words and two new content words you learned from your reading by using the Word Learning Tip and Vocabulary Building Strategy.

Put Words Into Action

ancestor **contribution** **culture** **newcomer** **tradition**

Directions Read the information in the sentences below. Then choose the word that best completes each sentence. Write the word in the blank.

1. In 1923 Duke Ellington wrote many successful songs. Some of them followed a very old African-American musical ______________________ (*ancestor, newcomer, tradition*) that had been passed down. It is named "call and response."
2. In 1929 Juan Tizol, a ______________________ (*contribution, culture, newcomer*) who was born in Puerto Rico, joined the Ellington band.
3. Duke Ellington was born in Washington, D.C., in 1899. Growing up, he learned about his ______________________ (s) (*ancestor, contribution, newcomer*) who lived in Africa a long time ago.
4. In 1969 Ellington received the Presidential Medal of Honor for his many ______________________ (s) (*contribution, tradition, ancestor*) to American music.
5. In 1986 the U.S. Postal Service issued a stamp to honor the many contributions of Duke Ellington to American ______________________ (*culture, ancestor, newcomer*).

Directions Use the above information to complete a time line about Duke Ellington. Write the correct vocabulary words in the blanks.

1899	1929	1986
Ellington is born. Growing up, he learns about his (**6**)________________ (s).	Juan Tizol joins the Duke Ellington band. He is (**7**) a ________________.	The U.S. Postal Service honors Ellington's contributions to American (**8**) ________________.

Create a Time Line With a partner, discuss people who have made important contributions to American culture. Choose one. Research his or her life and create a time line on a separate piece of paper. Use at least two vocabulary words and three new content words.

Review and Extend

ancestor **contribution** **culture** **newcomer** **tradition**

BONUS WORDS Here are two new words about coming to a new land. Remember that these words deal with the same big idea as your vocabulary words.

explorer someone who travels to discover what a place is like

individual a person

Directions Read each question below. Use the vocabulary word(s) in your answer. Write your answer in the blank.

1. What activities do you think a **newcomer** to America would like to do?

____

2. It is a **tradition** in the U.S. to celebrate the 4th of July. What activities take place on that day?

____

3. What characteristics do you think a person must have to become an **explorer**?

____

4. Why is it important to respect the **contributions** of **individuals** from every culture?

____

5. If you could make any **contribution** to American **culture**, what would it be?

____

6. What do you think your **ancestors** would think about life in the United States today?

____

Explore a New Place Work with a partner. Discuss and read about places you would like to visit or explore, where you would be a newcomer. Then write a paragraph in your personal word journal that tells about the place you want to explore and why. Use at least two vocabulary words and two new content words that you learned by using the Word Learning Tip and Vocabulary Building Strategy.

Check Your Mastery

Directions Circle the letter of each correct answer.

1. Which of these is not considered part of a country's **culture**?
   A. music B. art C. food D. mountains

2. Which of the following people is an **ancestor**?
   A. brother B. sister C. cousin D. great-grandmother

3. Which of the following is not a **contribution** people coming to America have made?
   A. written books
   B. performed music
   C. bought sandwiches
   D. opened restaurants

4. Which of these is not a place a **newcomer** to the United States would be from?
   A. Ohio B. India C. Vietnam D. Mexico

5. It is a **tradition** to observe Memorial Day every year. Which one of these activities might people do to observe Memorial Day?
   A. go to a parade B. go to school C. take a test D. go to work

Directions Complete each item with the correct vocabulary word. Write the word in the blank.

6. Making quilts is a ____________________ that is passed down.

7. Many states' names come from Native American words. That is one very important ____________________ that Native Americans have made to the American culture.

8. A ____________________ to the U.S. is often homesick for his or her country at first.

9. Baseball, jazz, and theme parks are all a part of American ____________________ .

10. Sometimes individuals know a lot about their ____________________ (s) because people pass down stories about family members who lived a long time ago.

Learn Words About a New Subject

Vocabulary Words

define **select**
example **summary**
opposite

Word Learning Tip!

When you read about a new subject, you may see words you have not seen before in your everyday reading. These words are often the longest and most difficult in the text. They tell you something specific about the subject. To learn these new words, think about the big idea or subject. In this lesson, all of the words relate to the topic of taking tests.

Vocabulary Building Strategy

Make connections between the unknown word and the big idea or subject. The new word will tell something specific about that big idea or subject. Tie together the big idea and the meanings of other content words that you know in the text. This will help you determine the exact meaning of the unknown content words.

Directions As you read the test directions, think about what you know about taking tests. What do the boldface content words tell you to do exactly? Think about how they relate to the big idea of test-taking.

This key word tells you to give the meaning of something, often a word.

Define each word below.

aquarium a glass tank in which to keep tropical fish

computer an electronic machine that stores and retrieves information

This important word asks you to name something that is typical of a larger group of things.

Name one **example** of a bird. Write the name of the bird in the blank.

sparrow

Learn Words About a New Subject

This key word tells you to find the word that has a completely different meaning than another word.

Which word has the **opposite** meaning of *dry*? Fill in the circle.

- ○ hard
- ○ soft
- ● wet
- ○ warm

This important word tells you to choose the correct answer from several choices.

Select the correct word to complete the sentence. Write it in the blank.

Lucy ___swam___ (*fell, climbed, swam*) across the pond.

This is a word that tells you to write a short statement that tells the main points of something written or said.

Write a **summary** of the fable "The Tortoise and the Hare."

A tortoise and hare have a race. The hare is so sure he will win that he takes a nap along the way. He forgets to wake up in time so the tortoise wins.

Connect Words and Meanings

define **example** **opposite** **select** **summary**

Directions Match each definition to the correct vocabulary word. Write the letter of the definition in the blank next to the correct vocabulary word. You may use a dictionary or the glossary to help you.

1. ________ select		**A.** to tell the meaning of
2. ________ example		**B.** a short statement that gives the main points but leaves out unimportant details
3. ________ summary		**C.** completely different
4. ________ define		**D.** to choose or pick
5. ________ opposite		**E.** something typical of a larger group of things

Directions Read each clue. Then write the vocabulary word that best fits in the blank.

6. A raccoon is a(n) ________________ of a mammal.

7. *Right* is the ________________ of *left*.

8. My dictionary ________________ (s) the word *grasshopper* as "an insect that eats plants and has long back legs."

9. Deborah wrote a ________________ of her favorite fantasy story, "The Night of a Million Stars," for a homework assignment.

10. Jake must ________________ the correct word from the three choices to complete the sentence.

Learn What *Example* Means Work with a partner. Choose a category, such as hobbies, insects, or sports. Write it in the center of a word web. Think of as many words that are examples of your word choice as possible. Write them in the other circles. Add more circles if you need to.

Use Content Words

define **example** **opposite** **select** **summary**

Directions Read each test-taking direction. Use the boldface words as a clue to help you rewrite the direction using a vocabulary word. Use each word only once.

1. Name a word that is **completely different** from the word *ancient*.

 ____

2. Write the **meaning** of the word *soccer*.

 ____

3. Write **the important events** of the story you have just read.

 ____

4. **Choose** the word that has the same meaning as *quick*.

 A. thick B. easy C. fast D. slow

 ____

5. Name **a kind** of musical instrument.

 ____

Directions Each item below is the answer to a test question. Use the underlined word to write the question that goes with each answer..

6. **Answer:** peas, green beans, broccoli, corn

 Question: (use <u>example</u>) ______________________________

7. **Answer:** This folktale about Anansi, the trickster spider, tells about how he tries to trick a rabbit. He doesn't succeed, though. In the end, the rabbit tricks Anansi.

 Question: (use <u>summary</u>) ______________________________

8. **Answer:** Lavender is a plant with pale purple flowers.

 Question: (use <u>define</u>) ______________________________

Write a Test With a partner, choose and research a subject, such as how to play soccer or Native American tribes of the Southwest. Use a dictionary or a textbook to help you. Spend a few minutes discussing the topic. Then write five items that might appear on test. Use each vocabulary word once.

Put Words Into Action

define **example** **opposite** **select** **summary**

Directions Read each item. Choose a vocabulary word that best completes each sentence. Write the word in the blank.

1. Yesterday, Sam and Mandy paddled their canoe up the river to see the beaver dam. A canoe is a(n) ______________________ of one kind of boat.

2. Some planets in our solar system are very warm, while others are very cold. The ______________________ of *warm* is *cold*.

3. If you have to ______________________ a word you don't know, you can look it up in a dictionary!

4. Julia decided to choose the word *orchestra* to complete the sentence. Which word would you ______________________ from the choices?

5. After you read each chapter of "The Moondancers," write a short ______________________ of it for your report to the book club.

6. Chris chose the word *lizard* as an ______________________ of one kind of *reptile*.

7. When you write a ______________________ of a book for a book report, you tell only the most important things that happen in it.

8. Sean will ______________________ the word *sequoia* as a giant evergreen tree that grows mostly in California.

Learn What *Define* Means List five interesting words. Ask your partner to define the words in a sentence. For example: *Ladybug*—A ladybug is a small beetle that usually has orange wings and black spots. Then, write a sentence that explains the difference between *define* and *example*.

Review and Extend

define **example** **opposite** **select** **summary**

BONUS WORDS Here are two new words about taking a test. Remember that these words deal with the same big idea as your vocabulary words.

continue to go on doing something

list a series of names, items, events, or numbers; to write a series of names, items, events, or numbers

Directions Complete each item with a content or bonus word. Write the word in the blank.

1. Create a ____________________ of four words that have the same meaning as *huge*.

2. How would you ____________________ the word *monitor*?

3. After you have finished this section of the test, ____________________ by going on to the next section.

4. Which of the pictures is an ____________________ of an animal that has fur?

5. A ____________________ should tell only the most important events in a story.

6. What is an example of a *vehicle*? Which would you ____________________ from the list?

calculator **flashlight** **computer** **tractor**

Learn What *List* Means Work in small groups. You have five minutes to list as many different things that you could do better by "making a list." For example, you could write "I could make a list before school to be sure that I bring everything I need." Members of each group should combine their lists and post a group list on the wall.

Check Your Mastery

Directions Choose the correct word to complete the sentences. Write the words in the blanks.

Louisa is taking a reading test. She had to read a short story. Then she had to write a (**1**)____________________ (*select, define, summary*) of the story.

Nat took a science test. In the first part, he had to (**2**)____________________ (*summary, define, opposite*) what the word *insect* means. Then he had to name a(n) (**3**)____________________ (*example, select, summary*) of a kind of insect.

Rosa took a spelling test. In the first part, she had to read a list of words. For each word, she had to write a word that had the (**4**)____________________ (*opposite, define, summary*) or completely different meaning of each word. In the second part, there were unfinished sentences with three word choices. Rosa had to (**5**)____________________ (*summary, define, select*) the correct word to complete each sentence.

Directions Complete each item with the correct vocabulary word. Write the word in the blank.

6. Please ____________________ the word *tarantula*, so that I know what it means.

7. Can you find a(n) ____________________ of a tool among these words?

A. telephone **B.** hammer **C.** bucket **D.** desk lamp

8. The ____________________ of *whisper* is *yell*.

9. The back cover of the book contained a ____________________ of the novel. Reading about the key events made me want to read the book.

10. You would ____________________ one of the following words to describe a character who is not friendly.

A. curious **B.** nosy **C.** unfriendly **D.** funny

Words and Their Histories

Read Words in Context

Vocabulary Words

ah	croak
boom	gurgle
buzz	hush
clang	ping
creak	screech

Word Learning Tip!

Some people believe that the first words people spoke imitated sounds they heard. For this reason, for some words in our language, saying a word out loud and hearing how it sounds can help you understand its meaning. The words in this lesson sound like their meanings.

Vocabulary Building Strategy

When you "sound out" a word and it sounds like a sound you have heard before, think about the meaning of this sound that the word makes. The sound of such words are what this word means. These words are called onomatopoeia words.

Fluffy's Rescue

"**Hush**! Let's be quiet," Marco whispered to his friend, Fred. They were walking into the yard of the old empty house on the corner. Marco's cat, Fluffy, was lost again. Marco hadn't seen Fluffy in a week. Fred thought that he'd seen Fluffy run into the old house yesterday.

Marco pushed open the gate. It was so old and rusty that it squeaked and **creaked**. Suddenly, it shut behind them with a loud **clang**. Marco and Fred jumped.

It was windy and almost dark. There were all kinds of funny noises. Whoosh! went the wind. Snap! went a tree branch. Crunch! went the grass under their feet. Water sputtered its way down an old leaky pipe into a birdbath. There were no birds though, and no Fluffy. A huge frog leaped out of the birdbath. It just missed Marco's head. Marco shook as the frog **croaked** over and over again as it hopped towards Grackle's Brook, which was **gurgling** in the distance. Then, Fred noticed a wasp's nest. He thought it was empty. He tapped it with a stick. In no time, they were surrounded by hundreds of angry **buzzing** wasps. Buzz, buzz, buzz, the wasps filled the air with their humming sound.

"Yikes! This is horrible!" **screeched** Marco as they ran to the back porch.

Then pebbles started to fall off the roof. The pebbles hit a bunch of cans. **Ping! Ping! Ping!** Marco and Fred looked up. They were afraid of what they might see next!

"**Ah,** Fluffy, not again!" Fred screamed.

Just then, a voice **boomed** from the next yard. "Who's on that porch?" Fred looked up and was relieved. He recognized his neighbor. It was Mr. Jenkins.

"It's Fred, Mr. Jenkins. Fluffy's stuck on the roof again."

Connect Words and Meanings

ah	buzz	creak	gurgle	ping
boom	clang	croak	hush	screech

Directions Read each definition. Then circle the letter of the correct vocabulary word. You may use a dictionary or the glossary to help.

1. a sharp, high-pitched sound usually of metal hitting glass, or rain hitting glass or metal

A. gurgle **B.** hush **C.** ping

2. a sound that expresses surprise, delight, or dislike

A. boom **B.** ah **C.** buzz

3. a loud sharp ringing sound made by banging things

A. clang **B.** boom **C.** creak

4. a very loud, deep sound like a drum

A. croak **B.** ah **C.** boom

5. to make a shrill, high-pitched sound like some owls and birds

A. screech **B.** gurgle **C.** buzz

6. to make a grating or squeaky sound like a door's rusty hinges

A. hush **B.** creak **C.** gurgle

7. to make a deep, hoarse sound like frogs

A. boom **B.** creak **C.** croak

8. to make humming sounds like bees and other insects

A. clang **B.** ping **C.** buzz

9. to flow with a bubbling or rippling sound like a brook; to make a sound in the throat

A. gurgle **B.** boom **C.** hush

10. to stop from making noise; to make quiet or still

A. creak **B.** ah **C.** hush

Find More Words In the story that you read, "Fluffy's Rescue," did you find other onomatopoeia words? List as many as you can identify that are not on the vocabulary list and come up with a sentence that helps describe each sound.

Use Words in Context

ah	buzz	creak	gurgle	ping
boom	clang	croak	hush	screech

Directions Complete each sentence. Write the correct vocabulary word in the blank.

1. Frogs make a deep, hoarse sound. When you listen in the night, you hear them go ____________________ , ____________________ .

2. Mosquitoes and bees make humming sounds. When you listen, you seem to hear a lot of z's. They ____________________ .

3. Many owls shriek and cry out in a shrill, harsh manner. They ____________________ .

4. A brook makes a bubbling, or rippling sound as the water moves along over rocks. It ____________________ (s).

5. A cannon can make a very loud, deep sound. Cannons ____________________ .

6. Pans ____________________ when you hit them together. The sound is like *clash* and *bang* joined together.

7. When you hit a glass with a spoon, it goes ____________________ . This word sounds like *ring*.

8. When someone is talking loudly, and you'd like that person to be quiet, you might say: ____________________ . This word sounds soothing and calm.

9. If you see a beautiful rainbow, you might express delight by saying: ____________________ !

10. That old door always makes a sharp, squeaking sound when you open it. It ____________________ (s).

Write an Animal Poem With a partner, brainstorm some ideas for a poem about an animal. Experiment with some sound words that describe the sounds that the animal you've chosen makes. Try to use at least two vocabulary words along with other onomatopoeia words. You may even want to make up some words that sound like the animal. Write the poem in your personal word journal.

Put Words Into Action

ah	buzz	creak	gurgle	ping
boom	clang	croak	hush	screech

Directions Sort the vocabulary words. Some words can be written under more than one heading. Write the word in the blank under the correct heading. You do not have to fill all the blanks, but do make sure that you use each word at least once.

Sounds Animals/Insects Can Make

____
____
____
____
____

Sounds Machines Can Make

____
____
____
____
____

Sounds People Can Make

____
____
____
____
____

Loud Sounds

____
____
____
____
____

Soft Sounds

____
____
____
____
____

Write a Scary Story With a partner, create a scary short story. What sounds can you use that will make your story scary? What sounds startle or scare you? Write the story in your personal word journal. Use at least three vocabulary words and three new onomatopoeia (sound) words.

Review and Extend

ah	buzz	creak	gurgle	ping
boom	clang	croak	hush	screech

BONUS WORDS Here are some more words that sound like the things they describe:

purr to make a low, soft, murmuring sound such as a happy cat

hiss to make a sound like an "sss," like a snake makes when it is startled

mumble to speak quietly and unclearly with the mouth almost closed

whir to move or fly with a humming or buzzing sound; a humming or buzzing sound

Directions Read each item. Then answer the question. Use the boldface vocabulary word in your response.

1. You ask someone a question. The person **mumbles** the answer, and you don't hear it. What do you say? ____________________

2. You pet your cat. It **purrs**. What does this tell you?

____

3. You take a hike in the desert. You hear a snake **hiss**. What will you do?

____

4. You are in a movie theater talking with your friend. The person in front turns around and whispers, "**hush.**" What will you do? ____________________

5. You have a picnic by a pond. You hear a lot of **croaking** sounds. What do you think you may see if you look closely? ____________________

Directions Look at the words in the box. Read the sentence and match the sound word that it is probably describing. Write the word in the blank.

creak	whir	clang
screech	gurgle	

6. I am a helicopter taking off, and I make this sound. ____________________

7. I am an old window, and I make this noise when you open me. ____________________

8. I am a running river, and I make this sound. ____________________

9. I make this ringing sound when an iron gate slams shut. ____________________

10. I am a hawk circling high in the sky, and I make this sound. ____________________

Play a Sound Game With a partner, choose three vocabulary words or bonus onomatopoeia words and write them in your personal word journal. Then take turns imitating the animal sound while your partner names an animal that makes that sound.

Check Your Mastery

Directions Read each sound. Circle the letter of the thing that could make the sound.

1. **boom**
   A. wind blowing B. explosion C. rain falling D. ice cracking

2. **screech**
   A. a dog B. an owl C. a fish D. a horse

3. **buzz**
   A. a mosquito B. an elephant C. a lion D. a dog

4. **clang**
   A. strumming a guitar B. playing a flute C. hitting a drum D. crashing cymbals

5. **gurgle**
   A. a bouncing ball B. a leaky roof C. a running river D. popcorn popping

Directions Read each item. In the blank, write the vocabulary word that best fits the sentence.

ah	buzz	creak	gurgle	ping
boom	clang	croak	hush	screech

6. The doctor said, "Open your mouth and say '______________.'"

7. Jasper was trying to study. His sisters were talking. "Please ____________________, I'm working," he said.

8. It was raining very hard. Every time the raindrops hit the tin roof, Lena could hear those ____________________________ sounds she liked so much.

9. Alicia is very handy. She oiled the hinges on a door so that it would not ____________________________ anymore.

10. Kai has a sore throat. "I'm sorry if I __________________________ when I speak," he told his mom. "I sound like a frog!"

Read Words in Context

Vocabulary Words

pair	reel
pear	sight
plain	site
plane	stair
real	stare

Word Learning Tip!

English words come from many other languages. Some English words are pronounced the same but are spelled differently and have different meanings. Although they sound the same, they are really two different words. These words are called **homophones**.

Vocabulary Building Strategy

When words sound alike but are spelled differently and have different meanings, they are easy to confuse. Think about the context of the sentence to determine the correct homophone. You can also look at how the word is spelled. Both of these strategies can help you determine the meaning of the word and how it is used in a sentence.

Zoom Into the Future

Imagine this! You're sitting on a park bench in town eating a **pear**. You don't have a clue that you're about to step into the future. Suddenly, in **plain** view you see a robot walking by. He's really weird. You think that his **sight** isn't very good because he is wearing a **pair** of glasses. When you look closer, you see that his glasses are really super telescopes that zoom in and out. Whenever the robot wants to **stare** at something and make it closer, he pushes a button. Zoom! Zap! It's there right in front of him. Wow! He's just pushed the button and zoomed right up close on something in the airfield. You look closer to see what else is odd about him. There's a tiny spool, or **reel**, of wire attached to his left robotic arm. He uses the wire to grab onto things and pull them to him.

You can't take your eyes off him. He makes a sharp right at the corner and moves towards Mallory Air Field, a **site** that is part of the Science Museum. You follow him, and you step right into the future! Wow! This is incredible! It's amazing! Everywhere you look there are robots. Hundreds of them sending thought messages to each other. You see an abandoned jet, an old kind of **plane** that people used to fly. It's a microchip stand. Nearby, there's a giant spacecraft. You've never seen anything like it. All the robots are suspended in the air watching the spacecraft. Climbing up a huge **stair** to a platform, you see a pair of robots. This can't be **real**. It looks like the spacecraft is going to blast off any minute to a new space colony in an outer galaxy. You buy a tiny microchip. It recognizes your thoughts immediately and programs itself to take pictures when the spacecraft blasts off. You're ready to record the future.

Connect Words and Meanings

pair	plain	real	sight	stair
pear	plane	reel	site	stare

Directions Complete the puzzle. Each clue is a definition of a vocabulary word. Use a dictionary or the glossary to help you.

Across

2. to look directly at someone or something for a long time without moving your eyes *(from a German word that means "having eyes that don't move")*

3. the ability to see *(from an Old English word that means "act of seeing, thing seen")*

4. two things that match or go together *(from a Latin word that means "equal")*

6. a spool on which thread or film is wound *(from an Old English word that means "spool")*

7. a machine with wings that flies through the air; short for airplane *(from a Latin word that means "flat, level")*

Down

1. true and not imaginary *(from a Latin word meaning "thing")*

2. the place where something is or happens *(from a Latin word that means "place")*

3. one of a group of steps *(from a German word that means "to rise")*

5. easy to see or hear; easy to understand; flat area of land *(from a Latin word that means "flat, level")*

7. a juicy, sweet fruit *(from a Latin word that means "a sweet fruit")*

Write a Science-Fiction Tale/Tail! Work with a partner. Write/right a science-fiction tale (or is it tail?) to a friend on a separate piece of paper. Choose two homophones, and include them in your tale. Try to use a few new homophones, too.

Use Words in Context

pair	plain	real	sight	stair
pear	plane	reel	site	stare

Directions Choose the correct homophone to complete each item. Write the word in the blank.

real/reel

1. The wire on the old fishing ____________________ is very thin.
2. Briana lives in a ____________________ log cabin that was built by her great-grandfather.

sight/site

3. Plymouth Rock is the place, or ____________________ , where the Pilgrims first landed.
4. The Grand Canyon is a spectacular ____________________ to see!

pair/pear

5. Geraldo's favorite ____________________ of socks have purple and yellow stripes.
6. Lila likes to eat a juicy ____________________ for breakfast.

plain/plane

7. The old ____________________ has two sets of wings.
8. The elephants were in ____________________ view of the jeep.

stair/stare

9. She stopped on the ____________________ to rest before climbing up to the top.
10. Never ____________________ at the sun because it can hurt your eyes.

Make Up Word Riddles Work together in teams of three. Choose two vocabulary words and make up a riddle about the word. Ask a team volunteer to write the riddles on a piece of paper. Then challenge another team to answer your riddles.

Put Words Into Action

pair	**plain**	**real**	**sight**	**stair**
pear	**plane**	**reel**	**site**	**stare**

Directions Read each sentence. Is the underlined vocabulary word the correct word for each sentence? Check Yes or No. If the word is incorrect, write the correct vocabulary word in the blank.

	Yes	No	Correct Word
1. The <u>plain</u> from Boston landed on time.	____	____	________
2. Gettysburg was the <u>site</u> of a famous Civil War battle.	____	____	________
3. Nick picked a <u>pear</u> from the tree and ate it.	____	____	________
4. Film for movies used to be wound on a <u>real</u>.	____	____	________
5. Take the back <u>stares</u> to get to the second floor.	____	____	________
6. The story is <u>real</u> and not imaginary.	____	____	________
7. Phil has a new <u>pear</u> of boots.	____	____	________
8. It is not polite to <u>stare</u> at people for a long time.	____	____	________
9. There were huge herds of buffalo on the <u>plane</u>.	____	____	________
10. It was a funny <u>sight</u> to see the squealing monkeys.	____	____	________

Find New Homophones Read silently for twenty minutes. Pay close attention to any words that could be homophones. In your personal word journal, write these words and describe how you knew which meaning was correct.

Review and Extend

pair	plain	real	sight	stair
pear	plane	reel	site	stare

BONUS WORDS Here are more words that sound alike but are spelled differently and have different meanings.

hear to sense through your ears, to listen to
here in this place
pail a bucket
pale not bright, light in color

Directions Complete each item with the correct word. Write the word in the blank.

1. If you want to know more about life in the future, look on the Internet. You can find a web (*sight/site*) ____________ that will have information.
2. The ____________ was flat with blooming wildflowers for as far as the eye could see. (*plain/plane*)
3. That grizzly bear must have been a (*site/sight*) ____________ to see!
4. The hardships that Lewis and Clark faced on their expedition were (*real/reel*) ____________
5. Come (*hear/here*) ____________ and I can show you some old pictures!

Directions Read each item. Then name the place or thing. Write it in the blank.

6. a place you might climb a **stair** ____________
7. something you have a **pair** of ____________
8. something you can **hear** on a radio ____________
9. something you can carry in a **pail** ____________
10. something you see that has a **pale** color ____________

Complete the Rhyme Your teacher will write a rhyme on the board. Read the rhyme with a partner. First, find the new homophones in the rhyme. Then write a response from the *stair* to the *pear* that rhymes and uses the homophone for the word *fair*.

Check Your Mastery

Directions Complete each sentence. Write the correct homophone in each blank.

1. A fishing line is wound up around a ______________________________ (*real/reel*).

2. A ____________________________________ (*plain/plane*) needs a lot of gas to fly.

3. Jake bought a _____________________________________ (*pair/pear*) of red socks.

4. There is a vase of flowers on the top ____________________________ (*stair/stare*).

5. The muddy dog was a ________________________________ (*sight/site*) to see!

6. The little boy wants a _______________________________ (*real/reel*) bunny, not a stuffed one.

7. Marissa just bought a delicious ___________________________ (*pair/pear*) at the fruit stand.

8. Everyone met at the _______________________ (*sight/site*) of last year's concert by the lake.

9. The directions you wrote were _________________________ (*plain/plane*) and easy to follow.

10. I like to ________________ (*stair/stare*) at the ocean and watch the colors change.

Read Words in Context

Vocabulary Words

any way	dessert
anyway	raise
council	rise
counsel	than
desert	then

Word Learning Tip!

Some words are tricky. A word may look so much like another word or sound so much like it that it is easy to confuse the two words. Think about the meaning of each tricky word. Make sure you know which meaning fits in the sentence.

Vocabulary Building Strategy

When you see an unusual tricky word, look very carefully at the way it is spelled. Think of a clue in that word's spelling that you can use to remember what it means.

The Corn People

The Arizona **desert** is very dry and gets very little rain. It is a rough land to live in because there is little water. Long ago, Native Americans discovered ways to gather water to grow crops there.

The Anasazi Indians lived in Arizona thousands of years ago. They dug ditches to catch and store water. At each end of the ditches were gates. When it rained, the water in the ditch would **rise**. When the farmers wanted to water their crops, they would **raise** the gates. **Then** the water would run out and pour over their fields.

The Hopi Indians lived after the Anasazi. They discovered another way to grow crops. They noticed that the rain ran down small paths through hillside villages. **Anyway**, it was in these small paths that they planted corn.

Hopi people ate much more corn **than** any other food. Women dried corn on the roof. After the corn dried, they ground it into cornmeal. They used it to make tamales and many other dishes. They even used corn to make a **dessert** named *pikami*. This is a corn pudding.

Hopis went to their elders for **counsel** and advice. Many still do today. Elders are wise older people in the tribe. They listen to people's problems. They help in **any way** they can. They are often part of a tribal **council.** This is a group of people who guide the Hopi. These councils are a very important part of Hopi life.

Connect Words and Meanings

any way	council	desert	raise	than
anyway	counsel	dessert	rise	then

Directions Choose the vocabulary word for each definition. Then use the word to complete each sentence. You may use a dictionary or your glossary to help you.

1. **Definition:** advice or to give advice
   Janelle was grateful for Louisa's ______________________ and wise advice.
2. **Definition:** compared to; except, besides
   Estrella is taller ______________________ Abe.
3. **Definition:** a dry, sandy land that gets little rain
   The cactus plant grows in the ______________________ .
4. **Definition:** any chance; by any method
   Is there ______________________ that you can help me?
5. **Definition:** a group of people who help others and give advice
   Maria is a member of the school ______________________ .
6. **Definition:** a food at the end of a meal, such as cookies or pie
   We had peach pie for ______________________ .
7. **Definition:** to move upward; to stand or get up
   See the balloon ______________________ into the air.
8. **Definition:** next; after that; at that time
   First brush your teeth, and ______________________ go to bed.
9. **Definition:** anyhow, in any case
   I ran for the bus, but I missed it ______________________ .
10. **Definition:** to lift something up
    Please ______________________ your hand if you have a question.

Write About Word History The word *dessert* comes from an old French word that means "to clear the table." Think about this old meaning for the word *dessert.* How is it connected to the meaning of *dessert* today? Write your ideas in your personal word journal. Then describe how you can remember the difference between the words *dessert* and *desert.*

Use Words in Context

any way	council	desert	raise	than
anyway	counsel	dessert	rise	then

Directions Choose the correct vocabulary word to complete each sentence. The words in parentheses are a clue.

1. The Navajo Nation has more people ________________ (*compared to*) the Hopi Nation.

2. Part of the Navajo Nation is in a high ____________________ (*hot dry place*).

3. It is very beautiful to see the sun ____________________ (*move upward*) at this place.

4. Many Navajo ____________________ (*bring up and take care of*) goats and sheep. Others make beautiful silver jewelry.

5. Many Navajo seek ________________ (*advice*) from their elders, as they did long ago.

6. Is there ______________ (*any chance*) you might be able to go with me to Navajo Fair?

7. Let's tell our ideas to the ____________________ (*group of people*) when we get together next Saturday.

8. ___________ (*in any case*), I think that it is a good idea to write down all of our ideas.

9. First, let's go for a horseback ride, and ____________________ (*after that*) we can watch the women weaving baskets.

10. Let's have some Navajo fry bread for _________________________ (*a sweet treat*)!

Write About Council and Counsel Imagine what it would be like to be a member of a council. In your personal word journal, write about the kind of council you would join and why. Name three topics you would discuss. Tell what counsel you would give. Use at least three vocabulary words.

Put Words Into Action

any way	council	desert	raise	than
anyway	counsel	dessert	rise	then

Directions Choose the correct word. Write the word in the blank.

1. In the early 1920s, the Navajo Nation formed a ____________________ (*council, counsel*) to give them advice.

2. Many groups____________________ (*council, counsel*) others and give them advice.

3. Part of the Navajo Nation lives in the ____________________ (*dessert/desert*).

4. The Navajo Nation owns more land__________ (*than, then*) any other Indian nation.

5. Many Navajo people ____________________ (*raise, rise*) sheep and goats and grow vegetables. The word Navajo means "planters of huge fields."

6. Some Navajos still like to cook over open fires. You can see smoke ______________ (*rise, raise*) in the sky for miles around.

7. Every summer, there's a big pow wow in Window Rock, Arizona. Jose asked his uncle if there was ____________________ (*anyway, any way*) that he could go with him.

8. His uncle had planned to ask Jose to go to the pow wow ____________________ (*anyway, any way*).

9. Inez decided she would go to the dance contest first, and ____________________ (*than, then*) to the carnival.

10. Have you ever heard of the Navajo ____________________ (*dessert, desert*) called blue corn meal pudding?

Make a Rising and Raising Chart Work with a partner. On a sheet of paper, make two columns. Label one *rise* and the other *raise*. Imagine all the things that can rise and all the things that people can raise. List them in each column. Then, on the back of your paper, tell how you know whether to use the word *rise* or *raise*.

Review and Extend

any way	council	desert	raise	than
anyway	counsel	dessert	rise	then

BONUS WORDS Here are another pair of words that might be tricky. Look closely at how each is spelled and listen to how each is pronounced. Notice that they are different parts of speech.

lose a verb that means "to not have something anymore"

loose an adjective that means "not closed or attached firmly"

Directions Read each sentence. Then choose the correct word. Write it in the blank.

1. Be sure the lock isn't broken on that beautiful Zuni necklace. You don't want to ______________ (*loose, lose*) it.

2. The ______________ (*council, counsel*) voted that the rodeo would be in September this year.

3. The ______________ (*desert, dessert*) may look like an empty place, but it's not. There are many nuts and cactus fruits to eat.

4. Do you like this beaded belt buckle more ______________ (*than, then*) that one?

5. "Is there ______________ (*anyway, any way*) that Charlie can ride in the rodeo tonight?" his father asked.

6. This dress is very ______________ (*loose, lose*). It is not tight.

7. Benita couldn't go to the Basket Ceremony. It didn't matter, ______________ (*any way, anyway*). She really wanted to dance with her friends at the pow wow instead

8. That ______________ (*desert, dessert*) is my favorite because it is covered in honey!

Create Word Reminder Tips Work with a partner. Choose two pairs of tricky words. Talk about what they mean and how they are spelled. What tricks could you use to remember the words so you don't confuse them? In your personal word journal, write a few tips for you to remember how these words are spelled and what they mean.

Check Your Mastery

Directions Complete each sentence with the correct vocabulary word. Write the word in the blank.

1. "Please ________________ (*rise, raise*) from your seats when Mr. Loloma visits our class today," said Mrs. Garcia.

2. It is much warmer in the summer ________________ (*then, than*) in the winter.

3. Is there ________________ (*anyway, any way*) that you could help me carry these boxes?

4. First help your grandmother dye the yarn, and ________________ (*than, then*) you can play basketball with your friends.

5. Celia did not want to go to the party ________________ (*any way, anyway*), so she was not sad that she had to work.

Directions Write the correct vocabulary word to answer each question.

6. I am a place that is dry, hot, and dusty. It doesn't rain a lot here.
What word am I? ________________

7. I am delicious. Sometimes I can be a chocolate chip cookie. I am very good after lunch. What word am I? ________________

8. I am a suggestion. I can help you.
What word am I? ________________

9. I am a group of people. This group likes to look after the interests of a community.
What word am I? ________________

10. I might do this with my hand when I know the correct answer.
What word am I? ________________

Read Words in Context

Vocabulary Words

- a bird in the hand is worth two in the bush
- a feather in your cap
- a heart of gold
- a rotten egg
- actions speak louder than words
- back to square one
- drop the ball
- get cold feet
- get up on the wrong side of the bed
- lend a hand

Word Learning Tip!

Idioms are sayings or phrases whose words mean something different from what the words normally do. When put together, the words become an imaginative way of expressing an idea. For example, "get cold feet" doesn't mean you really have cold feet! It means that you are frightened. You are afraid to do something.

Vocabulary Building Strategy

When several words in a row do not make much sense, you could be reading an idiom. An idiom is a group of words with a special meaning. To learn the meaning, think about the overall picture the words create.

Maple Street's Block Party!

Jenny usually can't wait for the yearly block party. She likes to **lend a hand** by helping Mrs. Jackson. Mrs. Jackson has been organizing this block party for twenty years to make money for the local animal shelter.

Everyone says that Mrs. Jackson is so kind that she has a **heart of gold.** Mr. Williams used to organize the party, but one day he let everyone down by quitting suddenly. He just **dropped the ball**. Mrs. Jackson took charge immediately.

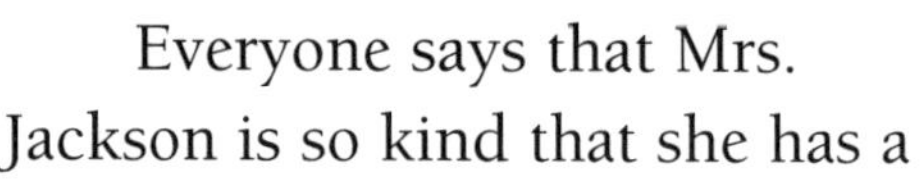

Today, Jenny was to help Mrs. Jackson. She was supposed to make a schedule of block party events, but Jenny **got up on the wrong side of the bed**. She was grouchy. She told her brother Charlie that she didn't feel like working on a schedule. He said: "Don't be **a rotten egg**! You'll spoil it for everyone."

"Can't you remember how to make a schedule?" he joked. "We can go **back to square one.** Let's have a quick make-a-schedule lesson!"

"You're so silly!" Jenny said. Then she laughed.

Charlie went on, "I think that you have **cold feet.** Mrs. Jackson wants to help you learn more about raising money for the shelter. Why would you risk losing this opportunity? You love animals! Just because Ralph told you that there might be a job at the nature community center, doesn't mean you should give up this opportunity. Remember that **a bird in the hand is worth two in the bush**.

"By the way, Jen, you should be very proud of yourself for all you've learned so far. It's a real **feather in your cap**. You always pretend that you don't care very much about helping out, but I know you do. After all, **actions speak louder than words**."

Connect Words and Meanings

- a bird in the hand is worth two in the bush
- a feather in your cap
- a heart of gold
- a rotten egg
- actions speak louder than words
- back to square one
- drop the ball
- get cold feet
- get up on the wrong side of the bed
- lend a hand

Directions Match the idiom in the left column with its correct meaning in the right column. Write the letter of the meaning next to the idiom. You may use the glossary to help you.

Vocabulary Words	Definition
_____ **1.** a feather in your cap	**A.** let people down by not following through
_____ **2.** a bird in the hand is worth two in the bush	**B.** don't give up something certain for something that may not happen
_____ **3.** a heart of gold	**C.** something to be proud of
_____ **4.** actions speak louder than words	**D.** to become frightened and back out
_____ **5.** get up on the wrong side of the bed	**E.** a person who does not act nicely and spoils it for others
_____ **6.** back to square one	**F.** be in a bad mood
_____ **7.** drop the ball	**G.** a very kind nature
_____ **8.** a rotten egg	**H.** be helpful
_____ **9.** get cold feet	**I.** what a person does shows what he or she is truly like
_____ **10.** lend a hand	**J.** start over

Create Idiom Cards Work with a partner to create idiom cards. On the front side, include the idiom and what it means. On the other side, draw a picture that shows what the idiom means. Play with another pair of students. Put the cards with the pictures facing up and take turns choosing a card and guessing which idiom it is.

Use Words in Context

- a bird in the hand is worth two in the bush
- a feather in your cap
- a heart of gold
- a rotten egg
- actions speak louder than words
- back to square one
- drop the ball
- get cold feet
- get up on the wrong side of the bed
- lend a hand

Directions Choose one of the idioms for each item. Write the idiom on the line. (Note: You might have to add -s to the verb to make it fit.)

1. Everyone on the team wanted to practice shooting baskets. Juanita said that she didn't want to. You might use this idiom to describe her: "You're being ______________________________. You want to spoil it for everyone."

2. Your sister woke up in a bad mood. You might use this idiom to ask her this question: "Did you ______________________________ this morning?"

3. Jessica has the lead in the school musical. She's thinking of quitting because she's too frightened to sing in public. You might use this idiom to describe the situation: "Jessica backs out because she ______________________________."

4. Mr. Chang wants two volunteers to help carry books to the library. He might use this idiom to make his request: "I'd like two students to ______________________________."

5. Derek completed a mathematics problem and discovered that it was incorrect. He might use this idiom to explain what he'll do next: "I have to go ______________________________ to find my error."

6. Mrs. Moore spent the last twenty-five years helping elderly people. You might use this idiom to describe her: "Mrs. Moore has ______________________________."

7. Your team just won the gymnastics competition. Your coach might use this idiom to describe the team's accomplishment: "This victory is ______________________________, and I'm very proud of you."

8. Mindy decides at the last minute not to play Queen Victoria in the play. The rest of the cast might say this idiom to her: "Don't ______________________________ now, or you'll really let us down."

Learn Other "Feather" Idioms Here are two more idioms that use the word *feather*: *feather your nest* and *knocked me over with a feather*. Choose one of them. Use a dictionary or the Internet to find its meaning. In your personal word journal, write a sentence using it.

Put Words Into Action

- a bird in the hand is worth two in the bush
- a feather in your cap
- a heart of gold
- a rotten egg
- actions speak louder than words
- back to square one
- drop the ball
- get cold feet
- get up on the wrong side of the bed
- lend a hand

Directions Read the sentences. Replace the words in boldface with the idiom that best fits. Write the idiom in the blank. (Note: You might have to add -s to the verb to make it fit.)

1. Every time I think about my dance recital solo, I **get so nervous** and I think I won't be able to go on stage. ______________________________

2. If you can **help us out**, it would be really great! ______________________________

3. If you **back out of this** now, we won't be able to play at the dance because we won't be able to find another drummer in time. ______________________________

4. Sometimes Julian is such **a bad sport** when he argues with the referees that it really annoys me. ______________________________

5. It's probably better to go **back to the beginning** than to try to find exactly where you made the mistake. ______________________________

6. I can't believe that you spent all weekend working on the report for us. It's really true that **you can tell what people are like by what they do**. ______________________________

7. Congratulations on winning first prize in the science fair at school. It is **a really good accomplishment**. ______________________________

8. Mandy was so helpful and friendly to all the new students this year. She has such **a generous personality**. ______________________________

9. Luke is so annoying and grouchy this morning. He sometimes seems to **wake up very cranky**. ______________________________

10. Are you sure that you don't want to keep your position as secretary of the drama club? You might not win the election for president. Remember, **don't give up something you have for something that might not happen**. ______________________________

Write a Story In the 1860s, Elijah McCoy invented many machines. His machines ran so smoothly that everyone wanted to buy them. People started to ask "Is it the real McCoy?" Through the years, "That's the real McCoy!" became a familiar idiom that means "That's the real thing!" Write a story in your personal word journal. Use this idiom and at least two others from this lesson.

Review and Extend

- a bird in the hand is worth two in the bush
- a feather in your cap
- a heart of gold
- a rotten egg
- actions speak louder than words
- back to square one
- drop the ball
- get cold feet
- get up on the wrong side of the bed
- lend a hand

BONUS IDIOMS Here are two other idioms and their meanings. Remember, you can't take the words at face value in an idiom. The expression has another meaning.

cover a lot of ground to make a certain amount of progress

hold your tongue to refrain from speaking

Directions Read each sentence. Then write the vocabulary or bonus idiom that best completes each sentence.

1. Chunan's mother said to him: "I know that you're disappointed about the trip, but I think it's a good idea to keep your thoughts to yourself and ______________________________ because your uncle is very upset right now."

2. Michelle was nervous about today's band rehearsal. The band has to rehearse ten songs. It is important that they ______________________ because the concert is in two days.

3. "That's ______________________________," Candace said to Lisa after she scored 10 points in the basketball championship.

4. Everyone on the team wanted to ______________________________ to help Tony hand out flyers for his band concert on Friday night.

5. Luis couldn't believe that the coach wanted Gary and him to go __________________ to revise their strategy for the basketball dunk contest.

6. Serena said, "Don't be such ______________________________. You'll spoil it for everyone if you don't come to the beach today."

7. Sally said she wanted to be in the play, but she didn't go to the audition. I guess that ______________________________.

8. Sometimes people are just grouchy because they ______________________________.

Create a New "Egg" Idiom Write a list of idioms that use the word egg in them in your personal word journal. For example, you might include on your list "don't put all your eggs in one basket," "good egg," or "egg on one's face." Next to each idiom, give a brief description of the idiom's meaning. Then create one new egg idiom. Add it to your list, along with its meaning.

Check Your Mastery

Directions Read each item. Then circle the letter of the idiom that best replaces the words in boldface type.

1. You learned how to read music very quickly. That's **a great success**!
A. lend a hand **B.** drop the ball **C.** a feather in your cap

2. Jenna was generous and good to everyone. She has **a kindness about her**.
A. a heart of gold **B.** a rotten egg **C.** a feather in your cap

3. Mrs. Jacobs said my story was excellent. I won't **get nervous** when she asks me to read it aloud to the class.
A. get cold feet **B.** actions speak louder than words **C.** a feather in my cap

4. Mr. Davis thought it was important that everybody **help out** so the school paper would get printed on time.
A. a heart of gold **B.** lend a hand **C.** a bird in the hand is worth two in the bush

5. "Do we really have to go **start at the beginning?**" Lilly exclaimed. "We worked so hard on this project."
A. back to square one **B.** drop the ball **C.** get up on the wrong side of the bed

6. "She's usually such a good sport. I wonder why she's being such **a bad sport** today?" Richard asked.
A. a heart of gold **B.** lend a hand **C.** a rotten egg

7. If you **don't do your part of the job**, we won't complete our report about why the butterflies return to same place every year.
A. drop the ball **B.** actions speak louder than words **C.** get cold feet

8. "Why did you **get up in such a bad mood** today? We're going to the beach for a picnic."
A. lend a hand **B.** get up on the wrong side of the bed **C.** a rotten egg

9. Your **behavior tells the whole story**. It's very clear that you don't want to go with us to the concert.
A. get cold feet **B.** back to square one **C.** actions speak louder than words

10. You have a great job! Don't quit it. You might not get hired for another job. Remember, **you don't want to give up a sure thing for something uncertain**.
A. drop the ball **B.** a bird in the hand is worth two in the bush **C.** a heart of gold

Glossary

A

a bird in the hand is worth two in the bush: don't give up something certain for something that may not happen

a feather in your cap: something to be proud of

a heart of gold: a very kind nature

a rotten egg: a person who does not act nicely and spoils it for others

above (uh-**buhv**) *preposition*: **1.** higher up than; **2.** on top of

abundant (uh-**bun**-duhnt) *adjective*: **1.** a large number; **2.** plenty

accept (ak-**sept**) *verb*: to take something that you are offered

acceptable (ak-**sept**-a-buhl) *adjective*: capable of being accepted

accident (**ak**-si-duhnt) *noun*: something not planned that may cause someone or something to be hurt

actions speak louder than words: what a person does shows what he or she is like

actual (**ak**-choo-uhl) *adjective*: real or true

adapt* (uh-**dapt**) *verb*: to change and adjust to certain conditions

admire (ad-**mire**) *verb*: to like and respect someone or something

adventure (ad-**ven**-chur) *noun*: an exciting time doing something unusual

after (**af**-tur) *preposition*: later than

ah (**ah**) *interjection*: a sound made to show such feelings as surprise, joy, or dislike—depending on the way it is said

although (*awl*-**THoh**) *conjunction*: in spite of

among (uh-**mung**) *preposition*: **1.** in the middle of; **2.** surrounded by

amusing (uh-**myooz**-ing) *adjective*: causing laughter or smiles; funny or humorous

ancestor (**an**-sess-tur) *noun*: a member of a family who lived a long time ago

angrily (**ang**-gri-lee) *adverb*: in an upset way

any way (**en**-ee **way**) *adverb*: any chance or any style

anyway (**en**-ee-*way*) *adverb*: anyhow, in any case

apart (uh-**part**) *adverb*: separated, not together

armchair (**arm**-*chair*) *noun*: a comfortable chair that lets you rest your arms

armload (**arm**-*load*) *noun*: an amount or load that can be carried in one arm

asleep (uh-**sleep**) *adjective*: in a state of sleep; sleeping

average (**av**-uh-rij) *adjective*: ordinary, usual, typical

B

back to square one: start over

before (bi-**for**) *preposition*: earlier or sooner than

behave (bi-**hayv**) *verb*: to act properly or well

beneath (bi-**neeth**) *preposition*: **1.** lower than; **2.** underneath

bleed (**bleed**) *verb*: to lose blood

boom (**boom**) *noun*: **1.** a very loud, deep sound; *verb*: **2.** to make this sound

break (**brayk**) *verb*: to damage something so that it is in pieces or no longer works

brilliant (**bril**-yuhnt) *adjective*: **1.** very smart; **2.** shining very brightly

building (**bil**-ding) *noun*: a large structure with walls and a roof

buzz (**buhz**) *noun*: **1.** the humming sound made by a bee; *verb*: **2.** to make this sound

* Bonus words

C

celebrate (**sel**-uh-brate) *verb*: to do something for a special occasion

chance (**chanss**) *noun*: **1.** the possibility of something happening; **2.** an opportunity to do something

chuckle (**chuh**-kuhl) *verb*: to make a sound to show that you think something is funny; laugh

clang (**clangh**) *noun*: **1.** a ringing, metallic sound; *verb*: **2.** to make this sound

comet (**kom**-it) *noun*: a bright object made up of ice, gas, and dust with a long tail of light

comfortable (**kuhm**-fur-tuh-buhl) *adjective*: feeling at ease or relaxed; cozy and snug

common (**kom**-uhn) *adjective*: ordinary, not special in any way

complete (kuhm-**pleet**) *adjective*: **1.** whole; **2.** has all the parts needed

continue* (kuhn-**tin**-yoo) *verb*: to go on doing something

contribution (kuhn-trib-**yoo**-shuhn) *noun*: something that is given

cooperate (koh-**op**-uh-rate) *verb*: to work together for the same purpose

council (**koun**-suhl) *noun*: a group of people who look after the interest of an organization or a community

counsel (**koun**-suhl) *noun*: **1.** advice; *verb*: **2.** to listen to people's problems and give advice

cover a lot of ground:* to make a certain amount of progress

cozy (**koh**-zee) *adjective*: feeling at ease or relaxed; comfortable or snug

creak (**creek**) *noun*: **1.** a squeaky, grating sound; *verb*: **2.** to make this sound

croak (**krohk**) *noun*: **1.** a deep, hoarse sound; *verb*: **2.** to make this sound

culture (**kuhl**-chur) *noun*: the arts, beliefs, and customs of a group of people

curious (**kyur**-ee-uhss) *adjective*: eager to know or find out

D

define (di-**fine**) *verb*: to explain the meaning of something

delicate (**del**-uh-kuht) *adjective*: **1.** very light and pleasant to taste or feel; **2.** finely made

delicious (di-**lish**-uhss) *adjective*: tasty, very pleasing to taste

dependable (di-**pend**-a-buhl) *adjective*: able to be depended on

desert (**dez**-urt) *noun*: **1.** a dry, sandy land that gets little rain; *verb*: **2.** to abandon someone or something (pronounced **di**-zurt)

dessert (di-**zurt**) *noun*: a food that is served at the end of a meal, such as ice cream or cake

discourage (diss-**kur**-ij) *verb*: to try to keep people from doing something

discovery (diss-**kuh**-vur-ee) *noun*: something that is found out or learned about for the first time

downside (**down**-*side*) *noun*: the lower side; the opposite of *upside*; **2.** a disadvantage or drawback; **3.** not the good part

drink (**dringk**) *verb*: to swallow a liquid, such as water

drop the ball: let people down by not following through

during (**du**-ring) *preposition*: within a period or span

E

easily (**ee**-zi-lee) *adverb*: in a way that is not difficult

enjoy (en-**joi**) *verb*: to get pleasure from doing something

* Bonus words

enjoyable (en-**joi**-a-buhl) *adjective*: being a source of pleasure

entire (en-**tire**) *adjective*: **1.** all of something; **2.** whole

environment (en-**vye**-ruhn-muhnt) *noun*: all of the natural world of land, sea, and air

example (eg-**zam**-puhl) *noun*: something typical of a larger group of things

explorer* (ek-**splor-ur**) *noun*: someone who travels to discover what a place is like

extra (**ek**-struh) *adjective*: more than the usual amount

F

faraway (**far**-uh-**way**) *adjective*: **1.** not close; **2.** distant

feel (**feel**) *verb*: **1.** to have a sensation or emotion; **2.** to touch something

field (**feeld**) *noun*: open land for playing sports or growing crops

fiercely (**fihrss**-lee) *adverb*: in a very strong or violent way

fight (**fite**) *verb*: **1.** to be in a battle; **2.** to have an argument

finally (**fye**-nuh-lee) *adverb*: **1.** the last; **2.** at the end

flat figure* (**flat**-*fig*-yur) *noun*: a figure that has only two dimensions—length and width

foolishly (**fool**-ish-lee) *adverb*: in a way that is not wise

fork (**fork**) *noun*: **1.** an instrument with prongs used for eating; **2.** a place where a road goes in two directions; **3.** a tool for lifting heavy objects

freeze (**freez**) *verb*: to become very cold

fresh (**fresh**) *adjective*: **1.** clean or new; **2.** not frozen or canned

friendship (**frend**-ship) *noun*: being friends; feeling warmth towards another person or people

funny (**fuh**-nee) *adjective*: causing laughter or smiles; amusing or humorous

G

galaxy (**gal**-uhk-see) *noun*: a large group of stars and planets

general (**jen**-ur-uhl) *adjective*: not detailed; applying to many things

gentleness (**jen**-tuhl-ness) *noun*: kindness, tenderness, and softness

get cold feet: to become frightened and back out

get up on the wrong side of the bed: be in a bad mood

gloomy (**gloo**-mee) *adjective*: dark, depressing, dreary, sad

grasslands (**grass**-*landz*) *noun*: large, open areas of grass, such as pasture or prairie

grateful (**grayt**-fuhl) *adjective*: thankful

group (**groop**) *noun*: a number of people or things that go together

gurgle (**gur**-guhl) *noun*: **1.** a low, bubbling sound; *verb*: **2.** to make this sound

H

habitat (**hab**-uh-*tat*) *noun*: the natural home of a group of plants and animals

handle (**han**-duhl) *noun*: **1.** the part used to carry an object; *verb*: **2.** to deal with someone or something

hear (**hihr**) *verb*: to listen to

here* (**hihr**) *noun*: in this place

hero (**hihr**-oh) *noun*: **1.** a brave or good person; **2.** the main person in a story

hexagon (**hek**-suh-*gon*) *noun*: a figure with six sides and six angles

hide (**hide**) *noun*: **1.** the skin of an animal; *verb*: **2.** to keep something secret or hidden

* Bonus words

hiss* (**hiss**) *verb*: to make a sound like an "sss", like a snake makes when it is startled

hobby (**hob**-ee) *noun*: something a person does for fun in free time

hold your tongue:* to refrain from speaking

horribly (**hor**-i-blee) *adverb*: **1.** in an awful way; **2.** in a way that causes fear

however (hou-**ev**-ur) *adverb*: on the other hand

humorous (**hyoo**-mur-uhss) *adjective*: causing laughter or smiles; amusing or funny

hush (**huhsh**) *noun*: **1.** stillness, quiet; *verb*: **2.** to make or become quiet

I

imagine (i-**maj**-uhn) *verb*: to picture something in your mind

individual* (*in*-duh-**vij**-oo-uuhl) *noun*: a person

instantly (**in**-stuhnt-lee) *adverb*: right away

interrupt (in-tuh-**rupt**) *verb*: **1.** to stop for a short period of time; **2.** to break in when someone else is talking or working

irreplaceable (ihr-i-**playss**-ay-buhl) *adjective*: not able to be replaced

J

judge (**juhj**) *noun*: **1.** someone who decides the winner of a contest; **2.** someone who decides whether someone is guilty

L

laugh (**laf**) *verb*: to make a sound to show that you think something is funny; chuckle

lawn (**lawn**) *noun*: an area by a house covered with grass

laziness (**lay**-zee-niss) *noun*: that feeling you have when you don't want to work or do much

lean (**leen**) *adjective*: **1.** slim and muscular; with little fat; *verb*: **2.** to bend over or rest against something

lend a hand: be helpful

likable (**lye**-kuh-buhl) *adjective*: easy to like

likewise (**like**-*wize*) *adverb*: **1.** also; **2.** in the same way

list* (**list**) *noun*: a series of names, items, events, or numbers; *verb*: **2.** to write a series of names, items, events, or numbers

lonesome (**lohn**-suhm) *adjective*: **1.** sad to be alone; **2.** not often visited by other people

loose* (**looss**) *adjective*: not closed or attached firmly

lose* (**looz**) *verb*: to not have something anymore

lunar* (**loo**-nur) *adjective*: having to do with the moon

M

mean (**meen**) *adjective*: **1.** not kind or nice; *verb*: **2.** to try to say something; intend; **3.** to be defined a certain way

meanwhile (**meen**-*wile*) *adverb*: at the same time

mine (**mine**) *noun*: **1.** a place beneath the ground where minerals are dug up; *pronoun*: **2.** belonging to me

misplace (miss-**playss**) *verb*: to put something somewhere and then forget where it is

mistreat (miss-**treet**) *verb*: to act badly toward someone or something

mistrust (miss-**truhst**) *verb*: **1.** to feel a lack of trust in someone or something; **2.** feel that something is wrong

misunderstand (*miss*-uhn-dur-**stand**) *verb*: to not understand correctly or get the wrong idea

mumble* (**muhm**-buhl) *verb*: to speak quietly and unclearly with the mouth closed

* Bonus words

N

natural (**nach**-ur-uhl) *adjective*: **1.** made by nature; **2.** normal or usual; **3.** not fake

neighbor (**nay**-bur) *noun*: a person who lives next door to you or near you

newcomer (**noo**-*kuhm*-ur) *noun*: someone who has come to a new place

newly (**noo**-lee) *adverb*: **1.** very recently; **2.** lately

O

octagon (**ok**-tuh-gon *or* **ok**-tuh-guhn) *noun*: a figure with eight sides and eight angles

only (**ohn**-lee) *adverb*: **1.** not more than; **2.** just one

opposite (**op**-uh-zit) *adjective*: different in all ways

orbit (**or**-bit) *verb*: to travel in a circle around a planet or the sun

otherwise (**uhTH**-ur-*wize*) *adverb*: in a different way

P

pail* (**payl**) *noun*: a bucket

pair (**pair**) *noun*: two things that match or go together

pale* (**payl**) *adjective*: not bright, light in color

pear (**pair**) *noun*: *a* juicy, sweet fruit

pentagon (**pen**-tuh-gon) *noun*: a figure with five sides and five angles

ping (**ping**) *noun*: **1.** a sharp high-pitched sound of metal hitting metal; *verb*: **2.** to make a short high-pitched sound

plain (**plane**) *noun*: **1.** a large area of flat land; *adjective*: **2.** simple, not fancy; **3.** easy to understand

plane (**plane**) *noun*: a machine with wings that flies through the air

planet (**plan**-it) *noun*: one of nine heavenly bodies that circle the sun

polygon* (**pol**-ee-gon) *noun*: a flat figure with three or more sides and angles

popular (**pop**-yuh-lur) *adjective*: liked by many

possible (**poss**-uh-buhl) *adjective*: might happen or be true

possibly (**poss**-i-blee) *adverb*: perhaps or maybe

powerful (**pou**-ur-fuhl) *adjective*: **1.** strong; **2.** having great power

prepaid (pree-**payd**) *adjective*: paid for or bought ahead of time

preschool (**pree-skool**) *noun*: a school children go to before starting elementary school

present (**prez**-uhnt) *noun*: **1.** a gift; **2.** the time that is happening now; (pri-**zent**) *verb*: **3.** to give something to someone

press (**press**) *noun*: **1.** the news media and the people who report the news; *verb*: **2.** to push firmly; **3.** to smooth out the wrinkles in something

preview (**pree**-vyoo) *noun*: something you see ahead of time

provide (pruh-**vide**) *verb*: to supply the things someone needs

purr* (**pur**) *verb*: to make a low, soft, murmuring sound such as a happy cat

R

raise (**rayz**) *noun*: **1.** an increase in pay; *verb*: **2.** to lift something up; **3.** to grow plants or bring up children or animals

real (**ree**-uhl *or* **reel**) *adjective*: true; not fake

recover (ri-**kuhv**-ur) *verb*: **1.** to cover again; **2.** to get something back; **3.** to get better after being sick

recovery (ri-**kuhv**-ur-ee) *noun*: **1.** the act of finding something that had been lost; **2.** coming back to health after sickness

* Bonus words

rectangle (**rek**-*tang*-guhl) *noun*: a figure with four sides and four angles

rediscover (ree-diss-**kuh**-vur) *verb*: to find again

reel (**reel**) *noun*: **1.** a spool on which film is wound; **2.** a dance; *verb*: **3.** to stagger

renew (ri-**noo** *or* ri-**nyoo**) *verb*: to make new or as new again; to begin again

renewal (ri-**noo**-uhl *or* ri-**nyoo**-uhl) *noun*: the act of making new or beginning again

replacement (ri-**playss**-muhnt) *noun*: **1.** the act of putting back in place; **2.** something that takes the place of something else

responsible (ri-**spon**-suh-buhl) *adjective*: **1.** able to be trusted; **2.** having the blame for something

reward (ri-**word**) *noun*: **1.** something received for doing something good or useful; *verb*: **2.** to give something to someone who has done a good deed

rise (**rize**) *verb*: **1.** to move upward; **2.** to stand up; **3.** to get out of bed

S

screech (**skreech**) *noun*: **1.** a shrill, harsh cry; *verb*: **2.** to make this sound

select (si-**lekt**) *verb*: choose

sensible (**sen**-suh-buhl) *adjective*: having the quality of someone who thinks carefully and doesn't do silly or dangerous things; **2.** showing good sense

service (**sur**-viss) *noun*: a kind of business or work that helps others

shine (**shine**) *verb*: **1.** to polish or rub something to make it bright; **2.** to give off light

sidebar (**side**-*bar*) *noun*: **1.** a short news story that is printed alongside a longer story. **2.** any information that is presented on the side of a printed page.

sidelines (**side**-*linez*) *noun, plural*: **1.** the area outside the borders of the playing field; **2.** activities other than a person's regular job

sidespin (**side**-*spin*) *noun*: a turning motion that spins a ball sideways

sidesplitting (**side**-*split*-ting) *adjective*: extremely funny; so funny it makes you feel as though your sides will split from laughing so hard

sidestep (**side**-*step*) *verb*: **1.** to step to one side; **2.** to get out of the way; **3.** to avoid or get away from

sidetrack (**side**-*trak*) *verb*: **1.** to move or distract someone from what he or she is doing; **2.** to turn aside from a main purpose or use

sidewalk (**side**-*wawk*) *noun*: a paved path along the side of a street

sidewinder (**side**-*winde*-ur) *noun*: a small rattlesnake that moves in a sideways, looping motion

sight (**site**) *noun*: **1.** the ability to see; **2.** something to see

similarly (sim-uh-**lur**-lee) *adverb*: in the same way

simple (**sim**-puhl) *adjective*: easy, not hard

site (**site**) *noun*: the place where something is or happens

sleepiness (**slee**-pee-ness) *noun*: the state or condition of being drowsy or ready to go to sleep

sleepless (**sleep**-less) *adjective*: not able to sleep

sleeplessness (**sleep**-less-ness) *noun*: the state or condition of not being able to sleep

sleepover (**sleep**-*oh*-vur) *noun*: an event where one or more people sleep at another person's home

sleepwalk (**sleep**-*wawk*) *verb*: to walk in your sleep

sleepwalker (**sleep**- *wawk*-ur) *noun*: a person who walks in his or her sleep

* Bonus words

sleepwear (**sleep**-*wair*) *noun*: clothing worn to sleep in

sleepy (**slee**-pee) *adjective*: feeling like sleeping or ready to sleep; drowsy

sleepyhead (**slee**-pee-*hed*) *noun*: **1.** a person who feels tired and ready to go to sleep; **2.** a person whose head is filled with sleep and not ready to wake up

snug (**snuhg**) *adjective*: feeling at ease or relaxed; cozy and comfortable

social (**soh**-shuhl) *adjective*: **1.** liking to be with other people; **2.** friendly

solar system* (**sol**-lur-*siss*-tuhm) *noun*: the sun and the bodies that move in orbit around it

soundproof (**sound**-*proof*) *adjective*: something that can keep sound out or is proof against sound

stair (**stair**) *noun*: one of a series of steps

stare (**stair**) *verb*: to look at someone or something for a long time without moving your eyes

summary (**suhm**-ur-ee) *noun*: a short statement that gives the main ideas

survive* (sur-**vive**) *verb*: **1.** to continue to live or exist; **2.** to stay alive through or after a dangerous event

sweep (**sweep**) *verb*: to clean with a broom or brush

swiftness (**swift**-niss) *noun*: the state of being very quick or fast

T

tabletop (**tay**-buhl-*top*) *noun*: the top of a table

telescope* (**tel**-uh-*skope*) *noun*: an instrument that makes faraway objects seem closer and larger, used to study faraway planets, stars and other objects

terribly (**ter**-i-blee) *adverb*: **1.** very much; **2.** in a way that is very bad or unpleasant

territory (**ter**-uh-tor-ee) *noun*: any large area of land

than (**THan**) *conjunction*: **1.** in comparison with; **2.** except, besides

then (**THen**) *noun*: **1.** that time; *adverb*: **2.** next; **3.** at that time; **4.** in that case, therefore

therefore (**THair**-*for*) *adverb*: **1.** as a result; **2.** for that reason

toward (**tord** *or* tuh-**word**) *preposition*: in the direction of

tradition (truh-**dish**-uhn) *noun*: something passed down, especially a custom, idea, or belief

triangle (**trye**-ang-guhl) *noun*: a figure with three sides and three angles

trust (**truhst**) *verb*: to believe in someone or have confidence in someone

tundra* (**tuhn**-druh) *noun*: a cold region, such as parts of Alaska, where there are no trees and the soil under the surface of the earth is always frozen

U

unannounced (uhn-uh-**nounss**-d) *adjective*: not named or told about ahead of time

uncomfortable (uhn-**kuhm**-fur-tuh-buhl) *adjective*: not feeling relaxed or at ease

under (**uhn**-dur) *preposition*: **1.** below; **2.** less than an amount

undiscovered (uhn-diss-**kuh**-vurd) *adjective*: not found; not known about

unfamiliar (*uhn*-fuh-**mil**-yur) *adjective*: not well known or easy to recognize

unimportant (*uhn*-im-**port**-uhnt) *adjective*: not of value or not to be taken seriously

universe (**yoo**-nuh-vurss) *noun*: everything that exists in space

until (uhn-**til**) *preposition*: up to the time of

upon (uh-**pon**) *preposition*: on

* Bonus words

upside (**uhp**-*side*) *noun*: **1.** the top side; **2.** an advantage or good part of doing or having something

useful (**yooss**-fuhl) *adjective*: **1.** helpful; **2.** can be used a lot

V

valuable (**val**-yoo-uh-buhl *or* **val**-yuh-buhl) *adjective*: **1.** worth a lot of money; **2.** treasured by someone or is important to someone

W

waterfall (**waw**-tur-*fawl*) *noun*: a stream of water that you see fall from a high place

waterproof (**waw**-tur-*proof*) *adjective*: something that can keep water out or is proof against water

wear (**wair**) *verb*: to be dressed in something or have something on

wetlands (**wet**-landz or **wet**-luhndz) *noun*: land where there is a lot of moisture in the soil, such as marshes and swamps

whir* (**wur**) *noun*: **1.** a humming or buzzing sound; *verb*: **2.** to move or fly with a humming or buzzing sound

wisely (**wize**-lee) *adverb*: in a smart way

within (wiTH-**in**) *preposition*: inside

without (wiTH-**out**) *preposition*: not having, lacking

workforce (**wurk**-*forss*) *noun*: a group or force of people that do work

workroom (**wurk**-*rum*) *noun*: a room where work is done

workshop (**wurk**-*shop*) *noun*: a room, shed, or shop where work such as making things or fixing things is done

worktable (**wurk**-tay-buhl) *noun*: a table on which you can work with tools

Y

yard (**yard**) *noun*: **1.** a unit of length equal to three feet; **2.** land around a house or building

young (**yuhng**) *adjective*: not old

* Bonus words

INDEX